MARCO ⊕ POLO

Travel with **Insider Tips**

ROME

D0795274

SYMBOLS

INSIDER TIP	Insider Tip
★	Highlight
●●●●	Best of ...
☆	Scenic view
☺	Responsible travel: for ecological or fair trade aspects

PRICE CATEGORIES HOTELS

Expensive	over 180 euros
Moderate	100–180 euros
Budget	under 100 euros

Prices are for two people in a double room with breakfast

PRICE CATEGORIES RESTAURANTS

Expensive	over 35 euros
Moderate	20–35 euros
Budget	under 20 euros

Prices are for a starter and main course without drinks

On the cover: The road of catacombs p. 114 | A superb concert hall p. 98

CONTENTS

Shopping → p. 84

Entertainment → p. 92

Where to stay → p. 100

Street atlas → p. 134

DID YOU KNOW?
Keep fit! → p. 20
The Pope on the web → p. 57
Relax & enjoy → p. 70
Gourmet restaurants → p. 76
When in Rome... → p. 79
Local specialities → p. 80
Jazz in a tram → p. 98
Luxury hotels → p. 104
Books & films → p. 109
Currency converter → p. 123
Budgeting → p. 124
Weather in Rome → p. 126

MAPS IN THE GUIDEBOOK
(136 A1) Page numbers and coordinates refer to the street atlas and the map of Rome and surrounding area p. 146/147
(0) Site/address located off the map. Coordinates are also given for places that are not marked on the street atlas
A map of the rail network can be found inside the back cover
Forum Romanum → p. 34
Map of Via Appia Antica → p. 115

INSIDE BACK COVER:
PULL-OUT MAP →

PULL-OUT MAP 🗺
(🗺 A–B 2–3) Refers to the removable pull-out map

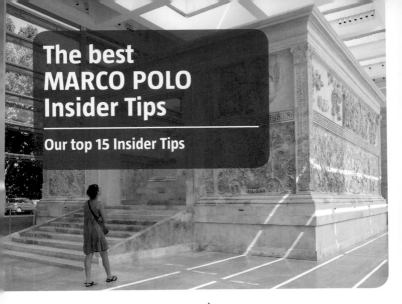

The best MARCO POLO Insider Tips

Our top 15 Insider Tips

INSIDER TIP ▶ **Home in Greece or Rome**
Legendary frescoes, mosaics and sculptures from the apartments of Empress Livia in Palazzo Massimo alle Terme → **p. 36**

INSIDER TIP ▶ **Cucinelli**
Brunello Cucinelli, prince of cashmere, patron of the arts and man of sustainable business, opened his new showcase boutique in Via Borgognona → **p. 89**

INSIDER TIP ▶ **Bio Bio Bar**
A star feature of the Casa delle Donne, the International House of Women, is the new vegetarian Bio Bio Bar in the garden – and during the day it's open for men → **p. 108**

INSIDER TIP ▶ **Sarcophagus dining**
Did all that walking along the Via Appia Antica make you hungry? Then stop at the Antica Hostaria L' Archeologia garden restaurant, where fountains splash, roses bloom and the pasta is wonderful → **p. 77**

INSIDER TIP ▶ **Dead poets**
Two English Romantic poets lie in the Protestant cemetery. John Keats arrived in Rome with an advanced case of tuberculosis and died there in 1821. Shelley was drowned in the Gulf of La Spezia the following year → **p. 63**

INSIDER TIP ▶ **View from a key position – the National Monument**
Residents of Rome refer to the bulky white monument to King Vittorio Emanuele II as 'the typewriter'. But from the top row of keys, the roof terrace at a height of 213 ft, you have a fantastic panoramic view of all periods of history → **p. 35**

INSIDER TIP ▶ **Stone gossips**
They may be carved in stone, but that doesn't stop the strange *statue parlanti* from talking. Once satirical verses criticising papal rulers were hung round their necks, and in the case of Pasquino the Romans still do this → **p. 116**

INSIDER TIP Nightlife on a hill of shards

In ancient times Testaccio was a rubbish tip where the Romans piled up the pottery shards of amphorae – they had no plastic or textile shopping bags. Today the *ragazzi* come here to give their all on the dance floor → **p. 92**

INSIDER TIP The ultimate sundown experience

Bring your day to a triumphant end on the Pincio hill admiring the sunset over Rome → **p. 51**

INSIDER TIP Glass-covered ancient monument

The 2000-year-old altar of peace, the Ara Pacis Augustae, is now protected by Richard Meier's ultra-modern glass roof (photo left) → **p. 48**

INSIDER TIP Original or copy?

If you think the glossy sheen of the equestrian statue on the Campidoglio looks too new, you are right (photo below). Corrosive exhaust gases were too much for the original Emperor Marcus Aurelius, and he rode off to the Musei Capitolini → **p. 35**

INSIDER TIP Picnic in the park

Gina, a high-class snack bar on Piazza di Spagna, will make you a gourmet picnic with salmon rolls, cheese, olives and wine, and all you have to do is find a nice spot in the park of Villa Borghese → **p. 78**

INSIDER TIP Fairy houses

The Coppedè quarter is like a fairy tale. The architect Gino Coppedè built wonderful villas and palazzi here in the early 20th century → **p. 66**

INSIDER TIP Optical illusion

The colonnade is not even 10 m long, but the effect is astounding: Borromini's play on perspective in the Galleria Spada → **p. 42**

INSIDER TIP Slow food, Roman-style

The pharmacist Giancarlo and his wife Nelly have a passion for old Roman recipes, and at Bocconcino, behind the Colosseo, they serve up seasonal dishes using regional products → **p. 79**

BEST OF ...

FOR FREE

● *Sistine Chapel for free*
If you want to see the world's largest art collection, Raphael's Stanze and the Sistine Chapel without paying a penny: on the last Sunday of the month there is free admission to the *Vatican Museums* → p. 36

● *Classical music in churches*
The view of the Baroque dome of *Sant'Ignazio* is confusing. It's a painted illusion, and nothing is real. By contrast the sound of the international choirs that you can enjoy there is authentic – and the seats at the back cost nothing (photo) → p. 46, 98

● *View of the Forum Romanum*
In Caesar's time Romans and travellers paid nothing to stroll across the *Forum Romanum*. Today you have to pay for admission, but if you just want to get a glimpse, there is a view from the steps to the left of the Campidoglio – at its best in the evening → p. 29

● *A train to the Mediterranean*
Rome's beach fans and clubbers know the way. The 20-mile trip on a local train to the beach resort of *Ostia* costs only 1 euro, next to nothing. Lovers of archaeology take the same train and get off at *Ostia Antica* to see a city of ruins → p. 71, 97

● *Arts week in spring*
Around Easter all of Italy celebrates the *Settimana della Cultura.* If you are lucky enough to be in Rome at this time you can visit all the sights, museums and galleries free of charge until late at night → p. 36

● *S. Pietro through the keyhole*
The Order of the Knights of St John, whose domicile is on the Piazza dei Cavalieri di Malta, boast an unusual attraction, and so far they are not charging a fee to see the surprising view of St Peter's Basilica that you get through the keyhole of the main entrance, the *Buco di Roma* → p. 63

●●●● Dots in guidebook refer to 'Best of ...' tips

ONLY IN ROME
Unique experiences

● *Drink from the fountain*

Eleven aqueducts kept ancient Rome well supplied with water, and free drinking water still bubbles from numerous *fontanelle,* the little fountains in the Centro Storico. So drink like the Romans: cover the jet with your hand and let the water spurt into your mouth from the upper hole → **p. 116**

● *Where politicians get their ice cream*

Rome has a dozen good ice-cream parlours, but *Giolitti* is a legend and not to be missed. No matter that the prices are eye-watering and the service rude: after heated debates nearby in parliament, Italian politicians of every party sneak off and cast their vote for one of their 40 kinds of cooling ice cream (photo) → **p. 75**

● *Step up, sit down*

Even if you've already seen a thousand photos of these gaily curving steps, the *Scalinata di Trinità dei Monti* remains one of the nicest and classiest places to sit and relax. People come here to flirt, laugh, take photos, meditate and dream the time away → **p. 53**

● *The mouth of truth*

All Romans who are newly in love make a trip to the ancient lie detector known as the *Bocca della Verità.* So far the man-sized marble face in the atrium of Santa Maria in Cosmedin has never really bitten off the hand of a beautiful woman who lied or a cynical macho – but you never know! → **p. 29**

● *Eat on the piazza*

In Trastevere there are still good ol' trattorias like *Da Augusto* on Piazza de'Renzi. There is no printed menu here, but the dishes of the day are chalked up on a blackboard by the door and everyone knows Augusto, who will come straight away with bread, water and the house wine, and take your order → **p. 79**

● *Campo de' Fiori: flower market and vanity fair*

Fewer and fewer of Rome's old market women now come to *Campo de' Fiori,* the city's most popular vegetable market, in the mornings. But this square attracts a fashionable crowd round the clock. It's a place to see and be seen → **p. 39**

ONLY IN

BEST OF ...

● *Galleria Alberto Sordi*

Who likes exclusive boutiques and beautiful cafés? For decades this Belle Époque building was in a dilapidated condition, but now it's a shopping arcade that can stand comparison with those in Milan → **p. 85**

● *MAXXImum contrast*

Rome's shockingly ultra-modern museum designed by Zaha Hadid lies between old barracks. The daring forms of this museum of contemporary art, known for short as *MAXXI*, will make you forget space and time (photo) → **p. 67**

● *Cappuccino with plaster casts*

The Romans like to drink their espresso at the counter, while the tourists prefer to sit outdoors. If it's drizzling, the *Atelier Canova Tadolini* in Via Babuini, once the studio of the sculptor Antonio Canova, is a charming place to take a *caffè* → **p. 74**

● *Down into the catacombs*

Explore miles of subterranean passages with grave niches that were hewn out of the tufa stone along the Via Appia Antica over 2000 years ago. The catacombs will keep you out of the rain while you examine the early history of Rome → **p. 115**

● *For chocoholics*

The trendy loft of the old *Said-Antica Fabbrica del Cioccolato* is where singles and couples come in all weathers to drink a cup of hot chocolate. If that doesn't satisfy your sweet tooth, you can buy delicious chocolate truffles by the entrance → **p. 75**

● *Tram trip with jazz concert*

Taking a trip by tram is an enjoyable way to stay dry, especially if you board the historic vehicle on a Saturday evening for a dinner with live jazz, as it rumbles from Porta Maggiore to the Colosseum, where you dine with a view of the arena → **p. 98**

RAIN

RELAX AND CHILL OUT
Take it easy and spoil yourself

● *A VIP spa for all*

At the *Benessere* spa in the five-star *De Russie* hotel you can relax cheek-by-jowl with Roman celebrities. There's a seawater jacuzzi, sauna and shiatsu treatments for the stars and normal mortals → **p. 70**

● *A wonderful piazza*

Footsore? Treat yourself to a *latte macchiato* with a view in one of the many cafés on *Piazza Navona* – a square for poor artists and wealthy show-offs, for people trading and strolling, a stage for activities that the river gods on Bernini's Fountain of Four Rivers have watched impassively for centuries (photo) → **p. 44**

● *Swim in the Eternal City*

Although the ancient Romans had a sophisticated culture of bathing, and architecture to match, today swimming baths are thin on the ground and overpriced. If you can't afford a dip in an exclusive pool in a luxury hotel, from June to September you can make your way to the *Piscina delle Rose* and also use the spa facilities while you are there → **p. 66**

● *Surf the book bar*

Book bars like *Emporio alla Pace* are all the rage. So when in Rome, do as the young Romans do and spend the morning sprawling in an armchair with a cappuccino and a newspaper, or surf the net all day long, and chill out in the evening with an aperitif and a few light bites to eat → **p. 75**

● *Relax for a midday break*

After all the sightseeing, something sensual might be tempting. Spoil yourself at the *Acanto Day Spa* with a 30-minute steam bath, an oriental snack and green tea. A nice time from 55 euros → **p. 70**

● *Night café*

It's the ideal combination of a coffee house and a Roman bar: round off the day with a cocktail in the ivy-covered *Caffè della Pace* in the company of Rome's elegant folk. Watch the world pass by outside and enjoy the dolce vita → **p. 94**

INTRODUCTION

DISCOVER ROME!

What is that man with the smart pith helmet and long white gloves doing in the middle of the chaotic roaring traffic of Piazza Venezia? He is leaning a little from the waist, has bent his arm and is pointing his hand like Michelangelo's Adam. An orchestra conductor in uniform. Will we hear violins starting to wail, the drums roll and an overture by Verdi begin? Troommh! No, nothing can be heard but a discordant droning of car engines, the buzzing of mopeds and the rattling of buses. They are going in all directions at the same time, and the piazza is gridlocked once again. 50 traffic offences clocked in spite of the new Italian highway regulations. Poor traffic conductor! If however you bear the madness on the roads with the necessary *pazienza,* patience, as the policeman does, and move on to sit on the wonderful Piazza Navona, where the waiter will serve you a creamy cappuccino and the obligatory glass of water with an elegant flourish, then you will realise that, for all its chaos, Rome is simply a fabulous place. And lots of things have improved there in recent years. The historic city centre, the Centro Storico, hasn't looked so splendid since the days of the Baroque

Photo: Scalinata di Trinità dei Monti – the Spanish Steps

architect Gianlorenzo Bernini. Soot-blackened façades have been made radiant with fresh paint, atmospheric pop concerts are held at the Colosseum and in the Circus Maximus, and the Galleria Borghese has been kissed awake from its long slumber after a 17-year restoration. Aphrodite and other divine sculptures are back where they belong in the new museums of antiquity, Palazzo Altemps and Palazzo Massimo. For the Foro Romano, the heart of ancient Rome, you have to pay an admission fee, but on some Sundays and holidays the Via dei Fori Imperiali and most of the Via Appia Antica are traffic-free, and walkers rejoice. Rome is wonderful!

Where Italians go about their favourite pastime

If you want to discover this city, you have to go out onto a piazza. For Romans it is a substitute for the *salotto*, the front room at home, as many of them live in noisy and uninviting places on the edge of the city or in cramped circumstances with their mother-in-law. But the piazza is where life is lived: it's a market, fair, a forum for gossip, demonstrations and religious services, a court where judgement is passed on matters of taste and a Circus Maximus of the vanities where the Italians pursue the pastime that is dearest to their hearts: cutting a *bella figura*. This means standing around with incomparable elegance, above all the banalities of everyday life, while keeping an eye open for good-looking female tourists.

In Rome there is a piazza to suit everyone. Pope Benedict XVI looks out onto the largest, most pompous and photogenic piazza, St Peter's Square – but for most Romans

The giant rotunda of the Pantheon: a pinnacle of classical architecture

Piazza Navona is a favourite place to meet and spend time: a long but enclosed open space, lively, colourful and intimate for all that. This Baroque stage for secular passions is however a work of the papacy, like many of the most decorative squares and streets in Rome. On the site of Emperor Domitian's arena for games, built in AD 86, Pope Innocent X had the Baroque *circo agonale* built in the 17th century, a name the locals corrupted to 'Navona'. Patricians and princes of the church took delight in the spectacle of furious contests from the windows of their palaces. Horses raced around the piazza circuit as in the Palio at Siena and bullfights were held in the classic manner. Long before Bernini created his Fountain of Four Rivers in the middle of the square, the Roman nobility staged water entertainments there with naval battles.

Today painters of kitsch display their sunrises and sunsets here, and artists will draw your portrait if you pay them a handsome price. A monsignore in black robes hurries over to the nearby S. Agostino church, two young nuns wearing flimsy sandals sit in the sun on a bench next to a white-haired man in a threadbare jacket and his mongrel. It could be a scene from a film. If you wait long enough you might see two carabinieri, a handsome man and a good-looking woman, ride past on well-groomed chestnut horses. The woman's hennaed ponytail, a perfect match for the colour of the horse, swishes behind her. The piazza is a place to see and be seen – and to enjoy life's cocktail, one sip at a time.

After dark the chic set of Rome gathers on Piazza della Rotonda in front of the Pantheon: stars and starlets, politicians and other VIPs wearing black shirts and white linen jackets for the summer heat, while teenagers and students, young men from

Roman stars, starlets and politicians

the concrete suburban wastelands on scooters, with their girls clinging to them riding pillion, come to Via del Seminario to get their *tramezzini* (sandwiches) and *panini* (rolls) before they sit around the fountain by the Pantheon.

Some people's favourite square is Campo de' Fiori, Rome's most colourful produce market, though sadly it is increasingly being taken over by clothes stalls. There are flowers here too, but the dominant smells in the air come from oranges, fish and seafood. Around Campo de' Fiori and in the narrow streets nearby there are lots of restaurants that give you a good meal and a good place to sit.

Rome's biggest village, Trastevere – the word means 'across the Tiber' – is worth a visit not only to dine in a trattoria. Even though Trastevere has been artificially smartened up since the 1950s and has lost much of its patina, you will still find leafy corners with splashing fountains, alley cats snoozing on walls and dustbins, and old residents who sit in their doorways on hot summer nights in dressing gown and slippers to have a chat.

But where is the Rome of the clergy to be found? Just behind the Pantheon, between the ivy-covered Piazza dei Caprettari and Piazza di Minerva, where a small elephant bears the weight of an outsized obelisk, in Via S. Caterina da Siena and Via dei Cestari. Here you will see the showrooms of clerical fashion. High-class shops sell everything that a pious fashionista could desire, from purple bishops' robes and grey underwear for nuns to well-cut soutanes and golden crucifixes.

If you haven't taken holy orders, you will probably prefer to hunt the latest fashions around Via del Corso, the Spanish Steps and Via Tritone, a kind of Bermuda Triangle where money disappears, though not without trace, in a stylish shopping spree in boutiques bearing all the big names from Armani to Zegna. The younger generation have got their own bargain fashion heaven on Via del Corso, where the latest music throbs while decisions are made about which cool leather jacket, jeans, skates or feather boa to buy.

Rome has 3000 years of history

But of course you haven't come to Rome only for the shopping. The Eternal City presents its 3000-year history in the shape of emperors' busts on the Capitoline hill, the Colosseum, Michelangelo's Moses and Bernini's Triton Fountain. You will be moved to tears – or possibly collapse from exhaustion – at the sight of the entwined figures of the antique Laocoön sculpture. You will find this amazing work about a mile and a half into the Musei Vaticani, which were designed to test tourists to destruction. You will gasp at the beauty, and the press of bodies, in Raphael's Stanze and the Sistine Chapel. Everyone should have the opportunity to see the Sistine Chapel, but since the huge restoration and cleaning programme that gave Michelangelo's smoke-blackened depiction of the Creation and his wonderful Last Judgement their bright and cheerful colours once again, the throngs of visitors have been so great that the idea of limiting numbers is now being considered.

And what about modern Rome? Contemporary architecture has a hard time of it in a city with a surfeit of Baroque palaces, where the marble, rubble and ruins of millennia are heaped up in layers. Until now avant-garde buildings of the kind seen in London, Paris or Berlin were regarded as an insult to the history and heritage of Rome. 'Everything that's new here first has to face comparison with Bernini's colonnades or the Colosseum', says Carlotta Mismetti Capua of the daily newspaper *La Repubblica*.

To see that a few architects have met this challenge, look no further than MAXXI, for example, Zaha Hadid's revolutionary museum for the 21st century in the Flaminio district. It seems to float like a summer cloud above the old barracks on the banks of the Tiber. Everything is in flow in this building. Even inside the museum, forms sway and swirl, staircases rear up as if in a cartoon film, gently sloping ramps appear and wedge-shaped corners lead visitors in new directions all the time. Renzo Piano's futuristic Parco della Musica auditorium, too, was not taken seriously at first, but now music lovers from around the world heap praise on it. The Romans have even

A romantic hour rowing in the park of Villa Borghese, Rome's green oasis

come to accept the modern structure above the ancient Ara Pacis, the altar of peace commissioned by Emperor Augustus, after Richard Meier, a star architect from New York, triggered off a cultural controversy in Rome with his design.

For all the progress, any died-in-the-wool *Romano Romano* – that's a 'Roman from Rome' as opposed to a immigrant to the city – will enthuse about how marvellous life in the capital of Italy was thirty

‚La dolce vita' at the Fontana di Trevi

or forty years ago, just as colourful, crazy and romantic as told in the films of Federico Fellini. On the day when Marcello Mastroianni died, even the foaming waters of the Fontana di Trevi fell silent, and mourning weeds were placed over the fountain where, in an immortal scene from Fellini's film 'La dolce vita' in 1960, the actor took a bath with the voluptuous Anita Ekberg. A bouquet of white roses floated on the water, and the sound of sobbing could be heard.

WHAT'S HOT

1 Arrivederci

Recycled bags Shop with a clear conscience. The bags designed by *Fendi* heir Ilaria Veturini Fendi are environmentally friendly and much more attractive than a jute carrier bag. Her designs sold under the *Carmina Campus* label re-use materials such as sunshades and hosepipes. You can buy them at *Re(f)use (Via Fontanella Borghese 40, www.carminacampus.org, photo)*. Green products are also on offer at *Momaboma*, where bags are made out of vintage magazines. And if you want to be cool in a colourful 50s look, call in at *Campanelli Katia (Via Lari 11, www.momaboma.it)*.

2 Monti

The trendy quarter of Monti is now trendier than ever. Rome's first *ice club* has opened here, with everything in it carved out of ice, so it is quite literally a cool location *(Via Madonna dei Monti 18/19, www.iceclubroma.it)*. To give yourself the right style for the nightlife, the place to go is *Contestarockhair*. This chain of hair salons has now opened a branch in Monti *(Via degli Zingari 9, www.contestarock.com, photo)*. If the business of looking beautiful gives you an appetite, satisfy it in Rome's most fashionable sushi bar: *Daruma Sushi Rione Monti (Via dei Serpenti 1, www.darumasushi.com)*.

3 Vatican by night

Nightseeing Get to see the Sistine Chapel and all the rest without jostling amongst crowds of sightseers. The way to do this is a night tour in a small group. *Italy With Us (www.italywithus.com)* run an after-hours tour, as do *Viator (www.viator.com)* and *Context Travel*, whose programme includes fairly comprehensive tours of the Vatican Museums after the normal closing time *(www.contexttravel.com, photo)*.

Lowbrow art

Everyday culture and anti-culture The latest trend on the art scene in Rome doesn't take itself too seriously. It aims to make art accessible for everyone, without gallery owners turning up their noses at the low quality of their visitors. To see work in the style of Pop Surrealism, go to the *Dorothy Circus Gallery* run by Alexandra Mazzanti and Jonathan Pannacciò *(Via dei Pettinari 76, www.dorothy circusgallery.com)*. Artists who work in this genre include Mauro Sgarbi *(www.maurosgarbi.com)* and Ania Tomickas, whose illustrations are displayed in the *Mondo Bizzarro Gallery* and elsewhere *(www.ania-tomicka. blogspot.com)*. An exciting contemporary art project that goes under the name of *MondoPOP* presents itself in the shape of a concept store that exhibits the creations of up-and-coming artists as well as established names in Pop Surrealism *(Via dei Greci 30, www.mondopop.it, photo)*.

Scents and sensibility

The world of perfume *L'Olfattorio Bar à Parfums* looks like a modern bar, but instead of a cocktail they will mix you a perfume. Roses, musk, sandalwood – sniff your way through some 200 samples and at the end you can combine them to make your very own personal scent *(Via Ripetta, www.olfattorio.it)*. Rome's first perfume gallery is called *Campomarzio70*. Here you can book a workshop to learn the art of creating perfume *(Via di Campo Marzio 70, www.campomarzio70.it, photo)*. If your nose prefers something more natural, follow it to the scent garden of *L'Orto Botanico di Roma*. This 30-acre botanical garden is a delight for all the senses *(Largo Cristina di Svezia 24)*.

IN A NUTSHELL

BENEDICT XVI

At the annual palm procession on St Peter's Square, the atmosphere is never less than jubilant. As always, olive trees adorn the piazza and thousands of admirers of Benedetto chant 'Viva il Papa!' But do the pilgrims remember what the Holy Father said about being the successor to St Peter when he was still just a cardinal? 'The nature of the office of pope is to carry the burden of others.' The pontifex maximus has seen the truth of his own words in recent years.

When Benedict XVI was elected in 2005, he was the first German pope for 500 years. At first the former Cardinal Joseph Ratzinger, who served for 24 years as an unbending defender of doctrine in the role of Prefect of the Sacred Congregation, surprised critics with his willingness to engage in dialogue. His liking for accessories like cool sunglasses or red custom-made shoes won him friends among the fashion-conscious people of Rome. However, the Catholic Church has been in the headlines for all the wrong reasons following the international scandal about paedophile priests, although Ratzinger himself had long campaigned to clean up the clergy. Benedict sees himself as a pope who 'wishes to intensify faith'. It remains to be seen whether he can find answers on such major issues as celibacy for priests, the ecumenical movement, homosexuality and contraception, which remained unresolved for 30 years under Pope John Paul II. Recently the Pope gave indications of a loosening of the church's condemnation of condoms, which some Catholics have interpreted as a sign of a liberal trend.

Photo: The colonnades on Piazza San Pietro

Viva Roma – some background on the passions and peculiarities of the city and its residents

CIAO, BAMBINI

Where have they all gone? Where is all the shouting and running around in backyards that was once as much a part of life in Rome as Vespa scooters, fountains and *gelato al limone?* The days when nappies were changed on the seats in church have passed. The clergy is aware of this: 'Romans, be fruitful and multiply. Have more children!' This appeal went out from Camillo Ruini, now the Emeritus Cardinal Vicar of Rome, some years ago. The retort of a Green politician was that the cardinal was like

a blind man speaking about colours. However, Don Camillo did have eyes to see, and it was obvious that in his prominent diocese there were more cats than kids playing in the back yards, that the lines of washing across alleyways were not hung with children's clothes, and that elderly signore were showing off fur coats rather than grandchildren when they went for a walk.

Italy is regarded as a child-friendly country, but it has one of the lowest birth rates in the world, and within Italy Rome, with a mere 1.1 births per woman of child-bearing age, is way down the rankings. Even though a family with lots of children remains a model in Italian society, in practice many young couples are reluctant to have more than one child.

The mundane reason for this is a striking lack of infrastructure. Child allowances, leave from work for parents, loans for families and tax breaks for those who have children are a distant dream. The same applies to good playgrounds, well-organised school sports or crèches and nursery schools. Only five per cent of children under three get a place in a nursery school. And the *nonna,* the grandmother who once lovingly gathered all the *bambini* to her skirts, isn't what she used to be: she goes out to work herself and has passed on her old job of child-minder to the television.

CINECITTÀ

The scene from La dolce vita is truly erotic. But on an ice-cold February night in 1960, when the great film star Marcello Mastroianni was due to get into the Fontana di Trevi with busty Anita Ekberg, life didn't seem so sweet to him. The blonde Swedish actress with the impressive cleavage was used to the chilly waters of the Baltic Sea, but her hot-blooded Latin lover went on strike on the edge of the fountain basin. The masterly director Federico Fellini couldn't film the sensual scene until he agreed to let his leading man wear hip-high angler's waders beneath his black trousers and dinner jacket – and then the myth of Rome as an international movie metropolis and city of party people was born.

Directors from the school of neo-Realism such as Roberto Rossellini, Vittorio de Sica and the grand old master Luchino Visconti had by then already brought new fame to Cinecittà, the film city founded by dictator Mussolini in 1937 for his own propaganda purposes. But it was Fellini, the little genius with the pepita hat, who became synonymous with the film studios on Via Tuscolana, where he set up almost all his bizarre erotic dream scenes: 25 films in almost 40 years, from La Strada to The Voice of the Moon, which was filmed three years before his death 1993.

KEEP FIT!

There is a lovely jogging route in the park of Villa Borghese: try running from the Galleria Borghese to the Pincio hill, from there to the church of Trinità dei Monti and back via Via Vittorio Veneto – or past the Galleria Nazionale d'Arte Moderna to the Etruscan museum in Villa Giulia, a distance of around three classically beautiful miles.

You can also explore the Centro Storico at a brisk pace by booking a personal trainer for a spot of *Sight Jogging*. The fit, multi-lingual city guides will jog with you along ten cultural routes through the city, even for early-bird tours at 6 or 7 in the morning, when the traffic is still tolerable. *70 euros per hour | tel. 0 34 73 35 31 85 | www.sightjogging.it.* If you prefer to cycle in Rome, there are now good opportunities: the new *pista ciclabile,* a bike path almost four miles long, runs right along the left bank of the Tiber from Ponte Risorgimento to Ponte Sublico. *Bike hire: Collalti Bici | closed Mon | Via del Pellegrino 82 | tel. 06 68 80 10 84*

Where men get passionate: Italians love their football, and some like to riot

After that it became quiet in Cinecittà. Not much happened there apart from one or two cult films: Gianni Moretti's Caro Diario and Giuseppe Tornatore's Cinema Paradiso. Many in Rome would like a return to the glory days, and since 2007 there has been a film festival in Villa Borghese each autumn. However, the shoots take place elsewhere, and even as classically a Roman film as Gladiator with Russell Crowe was not made in Cinecittà: Ouarzazate in Morocco was the preferred location. Arrivederci, Roma!

FOOTBALL

What do Italian men get passionate about nowadays? The right answer is: football, followed by football, and in third place football again. For a long time the king was Francesco Totti, captain of AS Roma. Scandals and manipulation of games robbed the Roman calcio of his innocence. Some sources of financing have dried up, and the clubs have their work cut out to tame their hooligan fans, improve the safety of stadiums and ensure higher standards of probity in their management.

Rome is fortunate to have the Stadio Olimpico, which is considered safe, and has two teams in Serie A, the top league: AS Roma and Lazio Roma. True tifosi have no choice in the question of which club they support: it is predetermined in their genes. A supporter of Lazio who dons a sky-blue scarf to go to the match on Sunday could hardly marry a woman from a red-and-yellow-clad clan that supports AS Roma. On the whole Lazio fans are from the suburbs, and supporters of AS Roma traditionally hail from the city centre.

Twice a year, for the derby match between the two rivals, Rome goes quiet. Then, after the final whistle in the Staby the Lazio fans, or for the south end where the *romanisti* wave their banners. For dates and information, see *www.ss-lazio.it*, *www.asroma.it*

LA MAMMA

Behind every fictional detective (*commissario*), politician, taxi driver or mafioso there is a *mamma* who looks after him his whole life long: 'We Italians are all *mammoni*, mother's boys', says Romano, an athletic-looking, grey-haired colonel in the Italian army. 'When things are difficult or I don't like what my wife is cooking, I go home to *mamma* straight away. She understands me. Always!'

Of course the stereotype figure of the 'mother hen' surrounded by her numerous brood has become rare in Rome as elsewhere, but the cult of mamma is stronger than ever. Because, in contrast to the situation in northern Europe, it's not a matter of chocolates and flowers once a year on Mother's Day, but of seeing *mamma* as the hub of daily existence. 'The bond between a mother and her son is a life-long relationship, and daughters-in-law can only get in the way,' explains a family therapist from Rome. She ought to know – her husband is a real *mammone*.

OBELISKS

Today tourists come back from Venice with models of gondolas, and from Paris with the Eiffel Tower. In the Caesars' day, however, one of the pencil-like, massive stone obelisks that the ancient Egyptians erected to honour their sun gods was the must-have trophy for a Roman general. Rome's most beautiful squares are adorned by twelve of them. The first was brought from Heliopolis by Augustus, and the last was looted from Axum in Ethiopia by Benito Mussolini in 1937 to add splendour to his residence, Villa Torlonia; it was returned spectacularly

Obelisks: stone souvenirs in ancient times

dio Olimpico, all hell breaks loose as the fans of the winning team go shouting and hooting their horns in a *corso* across the city. If you want to seize one of the remaining opportunities to see the stylish but aging hero of *AS Roma,* Francesco Totti, play in the seething cauldron of his home stadium, don't get a ticket for the *curva nord,* the end that's occupied in 2004. Many of these slender monuments are inscribed with hieroglyphs. If you should decide to go in search of these status symbols of the ancient world, you will be taking a tour of the best addresses in the city: they stand in front of St Peter's, the parliament and the Pantheon, on Piazza Navona and Piazza del Popolo, in front of the Quirinal Palace, the church of Santa Maria Maggiore and the Baths of Diocletian, high above the Spanish Steps and hidden away in the park of Villa Celimontana.

PAPAGALLI & PAPARAZZI

The dictionary will tell you that *papagallo* has three different meanings: a) parrot, b) pot for urinating, c) pestering admirer. In the 1960s the last of these three gained something like VIP status in Rome, when every pretty blonde or blue-eyed northern girl wanted to find out for herself whether what the magazines wrote was really true: that passionate *Latin lovers* awaited them by the Spanish Steps, softly breathing 'ciao bella' and 'ti amo' as they offered to show visiting beauties around one of the world's most seductive cities. Perhaps the *papagalli* deserve medals for their services to European unity: many a handsome *ragazzo* of those days is still attached to his blonde *amore*. *Papagalli* and *paparazzi* – hunters of skirts and celebrities – actually have little in common, except that they are both products of Federico Fellini's imagination. In the film La dolce vita the journalist Marcello (Mastroianni at his best) and his photographer, a man named Paparazzo, get into all sorts of trouble on Via Veneto – usually on the receiving end of Lex Barker's fists. This gave birth to the term 'paparazzo' for a tabloid photographer. The word entered more than one European language, as when a British tabloid

called the newly elected German pope 'Papa Ratzi', and to this day the *paparazzi* and *papagalli* remain hot on the trail of celebrity snaps and female tourists.

SCIPPATORI

Rome has famous artists and infamous artistes, the young *scippatori* or bag-snatchers. Two of them ride a Vespa scooter, one to steer and one to grab handbags in passing. If you have a gleaming new leather bag, leave it in your hotel room and bury your money deep in your pocket. Watch out too in the Metro, and above all on bus routes 40 and 64 from Stazione Termini to the Vatican, when young Roma girls with babies on their arm pass through and will skilfully relieve you of your wristwatch and wallet.

VATICAN

Once the Papal States covered much of central Italy, but now as a secular ruler the Pope only governs the world's smallest state. At 110 acres the *Stato della Città del Vaticano* is no bigger than a medium-sized farm and yet is the spiritual centre for a billion Roman Catholics. Some 600 citizens who carry a Vatican passport and 2000 Italian nationals who work there and cross the border every day are well cared-for. They don't even have to pay taxes, and a litre of petrol costs about one third less than it does in Rome. The clerical state has a 110-strong security force, the Swiss Guard, its own radio station for broadcasts in more than 45 languages, a supermarket, a railway station and a helipad for globetrotting popes. It also has its own coins, postage stamps and a bank whose cash points have been programmed to give instructions in Latin. It has almost everything that a normal state needs, even though the population is almost entirely male and the birth rate unsustainably low.

THE PERFECT DAY
Rome in 24 hours

`09:00am` A PANORAMIC VIEW TO START

Slept well? Camera at the ready? Then start the day by climbing the snow-white *Monumento Nazionale a Vittorio Emanuele II* → p. 35 on Piazza Venezia. On the right, walk up the steep steps to the church of Santa Maria in Aracoeli, then go left through a gate to the terrace of the monument, where the view is already worth seeing. However, to see an overwhelming panorama you first have to take the lift (7 euros) to the very topmost terrace on the level with the quadriga, where the domes, churches and palaces of Rome lie at your feet. Then treat yourself to a cappuccino in the *Café della Terrazza* by the lift.

`10:00am` UP TO THE CAPITOL

Descend via the church and then immediately go up on the right to the Capitol, the *Campidoglio* → p. 29 (photo left), where the Dioscuri Castor and Pollux will ceremoniously greet you. The statue on the piazza depicting Emperor Marcus Aurelius is only a copy. The original figure looks down majestically from his steed next door in the *Musei Capitolini* → p. 35, which you should not fail to visit – on another day.

`11:00am` WHERE CAESAR STROLLED

After passing the graceful bronze of the Capitoline wolf, who according to legend suckled Remus and Romulus, the founder of Rome, walk down the steps and take a first look at the Forum Romanum. Your journey through time begins now: from the entrance to the *Foro Romano* → p. 33 on Via dei Fori Imperiali you will reach the centre of power in the ancient world. Stroll as Caesar did along the Via Sacra to the Arch of Titus, beyond which you leave the forum again. Have you bought a combined ticket for the Forum and Colosseum? If so you won't have to queue for admission to the largest monument of Antiquity, the *Colosseo* → p. 30. Legionaries in historical costumes stand around waiting for you to point your camera.

`01:00pm` SLOW FOOD & ST PETER

Did ancient Rome give you an appetite? Then sample some Roman slow food in the trattoria *Il Bocconcino* → p. 79 in a quiet side street behind the Colosseum. But don't be too slow, because you have an appointment with St Peter. Take Metro B from the Colosseo two stops to Termini, and there take express bus no. 40 (Piazza

Get to know the best sides of Rome – in the thick of things, relaxed, in one day

Pia) or 64 (to Porta Cavalleggeri) direct to *San Pietro* → p. 61 (photo below left), Christendom's most imposing church. In front of it, on the ellipse-shaped *Piazza San Pietro* → p. 60 with its elegant colonnades desig-ned by Bernini, throngs of Catho-lics assemble every Wednesday for an audience with the Pope. To the right of the Vatican ensemble lies the entrance to the *Musei Vatica-ni* → p. 57 and the *Cappella Sistina* → p. 59, but you will need to schedule in an extra day to see them.

`04:00pm` CASTEL SANT'ANGELO & PIAZZA NAVONA

To reach *Castel Sant'Angelo* → p. 56 cross Via della Conciliazione. Inspired by Bernini's elegant statues of an-gels – and pestered by all the hawkers – you take Ponte Sant'Angelo across the Tiber back into the Centro Storico. Via dei Coronari, where you can buy a quick souvenir, a work of art or a fashion accessory, will lead you to the lively *Piazza Navona* → p. 44. If you are wilting by this stage, a *gelato* or *caffè* enjoyed among a colourful crowd of people will liven you up again.

`06:00pm` APERITIF ON CAMPO DE' FIORI

Stroll on to *Campo de' Fiori* → p. 39, where you can order an *aperitivo* and linger in wonderful surroundings until evening, as this is the rendezvous for Roman *ragazzi*. By 8pm the many trattorias of the district will be filling up. Have a meal at, e.g., *Pierluigi* → p. 78 on nearby Piazza dei Ricci (remember to book in advance!). After a good evening meal, walk over to Largo di Torre Argentina, a stop on the main bus routes.

`10:00pm` NIGHTLIFE IN TRASTEVERE

If you are still up for it, and not ready to go back to your hotel, catch tram no. 8 from Largo di Torre Argentina. It's a di-rect route to the nightlife of *Trastevere* → p. 92 (photo top), the district with the most clubs and nightspots.

Bus to the start: 30, 40, 85, 87, 119
Stop: Piazza Venezia
You can also do this tour by bike;
see p. 122 for rentals

SIGHTSEEING

CITY **WHERE TO START?**
 Largo di Torre Argentina **(137 D4)** *(ΜΙ F9)* is a good starting point for a first exploration of the historic city centre. From here it is no more than three minutes to **Piazza Navona** or ten minutes to **Campo de' Fiori** and your first cappuccino break of the day. To the east it takes only 15 minutes to walk to the Capitoline Hill or half an hour to the **Foro Romano** and **Colosseo**. Many buses stop at Largo di Torre Argentina, e.g. no. 60, 62, 63, 70, 81, 95; parking: Villa Borghese/Viale del Muro Torto **(140 A3)** *(ΜΙ F6)*

It's impossible to overlook the sights of Rome. And it's equally impossible to see all of them. In its 3000-year history the Eternal City has amassed so many treasures that no computer has catalogued all of them.

There are more churches than days in the year, each vying to surpass the others for opulence and beauty. The Pope is the vicar of the four patriarchal basilicas San Giovanni in Laterano, the mother church of Roman Catholics, San Pietro in Vaticano, i.e. St Peter's, Santa Maria Maggiore and San Paolo fuori le Mura. Pious visitors also try to fit in a visit to San Lorenzo, Santa Croce in Gerusalemme and San Sebastiano, which complete the array of seven pilgrimage churches.

Photo: San Pietro

Magnificent churches and palaces, ancient forums and catacombs – there is no end to Rome's cultural treasures

With all these heavenly treasures, it's easy to neglect worldly sights – and especially those of the underworld. Archaeologists are continually making exciting discoveries, such as the 2000-year-old Roman villa beneath the ultra-modern auditorium of the Parco della Musica; excavations will delay construction of the new Metro line on Piazza Venezia for years. There is good news to report, too: the ubiquitous signs saying 'chiuso per restauro' (closed for restoration) have become less common. The marble beauties of the ancient world have found a worthy residence in Palazzo Altemps and Palazzo Massimo. The Musei Capitolini, the world's oldest museums, have had a stylish refurbishment. And many works of art that moved temporarily to the former power station of Montemartini in Via Ostiense have been permitted to stay in their unusual home. Rome has regained its old splendour.

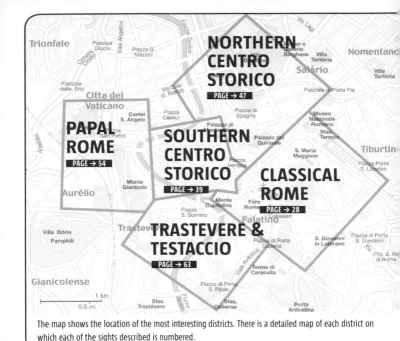

The map shows the location of the most interesting districts. There is a detailed map of each district on which each of the sights described is numbered.

CLASSICAL ROME

From the Capitol to the Lateran: Rome's early age of marble can be found here between the imperial forums, triumphal arches and the Colosseum, as well as one of the finest golden mosaics of the Middle Ages in Santa Prassede.

Close to the modern Stazione Termini you will also find the largest baths of ancient Roman times, the superb patriarchal basilica Santa Maria Maggiore and Michelangelo's majestic Moses. In Monti, as this lovely old quarter is called, you can take a trip back in time at every corner, down to the vaults of the lower church of San Clemente or up to the square at the Capitol. Monti really has everything: down-to-earth charm around Piazza Santa Maria in Monti, nightlife in Via dei Serpenti and from time to time a festival on the streets between the Colosseum and Capitol, when Via dei Fori Imperiali is closed to traffic.

■ ARCO DI COSTANTINO
(144 A2) (*∅ G10*)

The Arch of Constantine with its carved reliefs was erected next to the Colosseum after Emperor Constantine's victory at the Milvian Bridge (AD 312). This seems premature when you consider that Constantine had not conquered new lands or won a war, but merely defeated his opponent Maxentius. Reliefs from older monuments were appropriated for the decoration. *Piazza del Colosseo | Metro B: Colosseo*

2 BOCCA DELLA VERITÀ ●

(143 E3) (*E10*)

The 'mouth of truth' is a strange marble face as tall as a man on the left of the atrium of *Santa Maria in Cosmedin*. The left eye seems to be shedding tears, and only the mouth has been worn smooth, as visitors place their hands into the monster's jaws. By tradition jealous married people send their partners there. If they don't tell the truth, this ancient lie detector is said to bite off the hand. *Daily 9am–6pm, in winter 9am–5pm | Piazza Bocca della Verità | bus 63, 30, 160, 170, 628*

3 CAMPIDOGLIO ★

(137 E–F5–6) (*F9*)

Where the Temples of Jupiter and Juno once stood, in 1536 Michelangelo laid out the trapezium-shaped square of the Capitol, flanked by the *Palazzo dei Senatori*, the *Palazzo dei Conservatori* and the *Palazzo Nuovo*. The pedestal from which Emperor Marcus Aurelius greets passers-by with a raised hand today bears a copy of the original statue dating from the 2nd century, which needed protection from pollution and was moved inside the *Musei Capitolini*. ● If you take the steps to the left of the Piazza del Campidoglio, you have a wonderful view of the Foro Romano. *Piazza del Campidoglio | bus 30, 60, 62, 63, 64, 70, 81, 87, 117, 119, 160, 630*

4 CIRCO MASSIMO (143 F3) (*F10–11*)

2000 years ago courageous gladiators and daring chariot drivers were cheered by crowds here. Now the Circo Massimo is used for open-air concerts. The biggest racecourse in antiquity (*massimo* – large)

MARCO POLO HIGHLIGHTS

★ Campidoglio
Michelangelo's trapezium-shaped square on the Capitol → p. 29

★ Colosseo
Bread and circuses in the arena → p. 30

★ Foro Romano
Tread in the footsteps of Caesar and Cicero – the centre of power of the ancient world → p. 33

★ Musei Capitolini
Stars of antiquity: Venus, the Capitoline Wolf and the Dying Gaul → p. 35

★ Pantheon
A domed rotunda, one of the greatest architectural works of ancient Rome → p. 44

★ Piazza Navona
Strut on the finest Baroque stage → p. 44

★ Fontana di Trevi
Rome's favourite fountain → p. 50

★ Galleria Borghese
Bernini's sensual sculptures in a newly restored pleasure palace → p. 50

★ Cappella Sistina
Michelangelo's famous frescoes in the Musei Vaticani → p. 59

★ San Pietro
St Peter's Basilica: the heart of the Roman Catholic world → p. 61

★ Centrale Montemartini
Ancient sculptures in a power station → p. 66

★ MAXXI
Zaha Hadid's museum for contemporary art is a revolution in the Eternal City → p. 67

accommodated up to 300,000 people. Today it holds merely tens of thousands, and even from outside the arena you can clearly hear the melting Italian timbre of stars such as Eros Ramazzotti. *Via del Circo Massimo | Metro B: Circo Massimo, tram 3*

▪5 COLOSSEO ★ (144 A2) (*ω G10*)

There are good reasons why the Colosseum, the emblem of classical Rome, was again voted one of the 'seven new wonders of the world' in a global poll. Emperor Vespasian, the successor to cruel Nero, wanted to gain the admiration of the people by building this gigantic three-storey arcaded stadium to stage *panem et circenses*, bread and circuses, just as politicians do today when they bid to hold football championships and Olympic Games. What Vespasian started in AD 72, his son Titus completed in a sensational construction period of just eight years, even adding a fourth storey.

The amphitheatre held 50,000 spectators: the first three tiers were reserved for Roman notables, while women and plebeians crammed into the uppermost wooden gallery beneath the sails that kept off the sun. At the games lasting 100 days to inaugurate the Colosseum, countless gladiators and wild animals were slaughtered. Emperor Trajan (98–117) once commanded 5000 gladiators to appear. 'Ave Caesar, morituri te salutant' (Caesar, we who are about to die greet you) was their cry. Today the Colosseum is a memorial in opposition to the death penalty. Since 1999 it has been bathed in green light every time a death sentence somewhere in the world is not carried out or a state decides to abolish the death penalty. *Daily 9am until one hour before dusk (opening times may be restricted due to restoration work) | admission 12 euros (also valid for Foro Romano and Palatine) | Piazza del Colosseo | Metro B: Colosseo*

Only half of it survives, but it is still the largest building of ancient Rome: the Colosseo

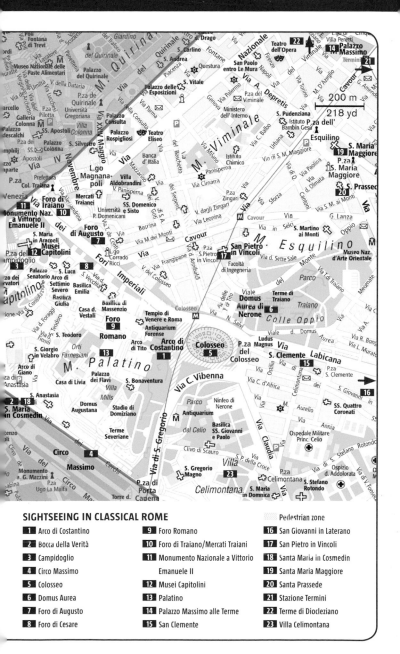

SIGHTSEEING IN CLASSICAL ROME

Pedestrian zone

1 Arco di Costantino
2 Bocca della Verità
3 Campidoglio
4 Circo Massimo
5 Colosseo
6 Domus Aurea
7 Foro di Augusto
8 Foro di Cesare

9 Foro Romano
10 Foro di Traiano/Mercati Traiani
11 Monumento Nazionale a Vittorio Emanuele II
12 Musei Capitolini
13 Palatino
14 Palazzo Massimo alle Terme
15 San Clemente

16 San Giovanni in Laterano
17 San Pietro in Vincoli
18 Santa Maria in Cosmedin
19 Santa Maria Maggiore
20 Santa Prassede
21 Stazione Termini
22 Terme di Diocleziano
23 Villa Celimontana

6 DOMUS AUREA (144 B2) *(🗺 G9)*
Emperor Nero (AD 54–68), who played with fire and crucified Christians, built the Golden House, the most expensive and the largest palace of the ancient world. Unfortunately little of it has survived. *Closed for restoration at present | Viale Domus Aurea | Metro B: Colosseo, bus 117*

7 FORO DI AUGUSTO
(144 A1) *(🗺 F9)*
The Forum of Augustus is dominated by the temple of the vengeful Roman god of war, Mars, and commemorates the Battle of Philippi (42 BC), at which Marc Antony and Octavian (the later Emperor Augustus) finally defeated Caesar's assassins. Augustus, the emperor of peace (27 BC – AD 14), had over 80 temples built or adorned. He is said to have found Rome built of brick and left it built of marble. There is a good view from 🔭 Via dei Fori Imperiali. *Piazzetta del Grillo | bus 85, 87, 117*

8 FORO DI CESARE (137 F5) *(🗺 F9)*
Caesar had the *Forum Julium,* as Caesar's Forum is properly known, built at his own expense. Still recognisable are the rows of shops, the remains of the Basilica Argentaria, which was used as a bank and exchange, and three surviving columns of the Temple of Venus. One day, as the historian Suetonius relates, the consul received the senate seated on the base of the Temple of Venus. With this affront to piety – only gods were allowed to sit – Caesar claimed a status equal to Jupiter. This happened shortly before he was

Foro Romano: the centre of power in the ancient world for almost 1000 years

murdered in 44 BC. *Via dei Fori Imperiali | bus 85, 87, 117, 175*

⑨ FORO ROMANO ★
(137 F5–6) *(𝄞 F9–10)*

From his office in Palazzo Senatorio in the Capitol, the mayor of Rome has the best view of the marble-clad centre of power in the ancient world. The Forum Romanum, originally conceived as a sanctuary of Vesta, evolved from a cattle market to a political arena from which not only Rome but the whole Roman Empire was ruled. This is where Cicero made his flaming orations against Catilina and old Cato spoke his *ceterum censeo:* 'Carthage must be destroyed.' Today you don't have to wear a toga to stroll between columns and triumphal arches on warm evenings: INSIDER TIP *Roma*

sotto le stelle (Rome beneath the stars) is the name for night tours *(in Italian and English | June–mid-Sept | dates from the tourist information pavilions and newspapers, e.g. La Repubblica)*.

Here are some highlights: From the entrance on Via dei Fori Imperiali you pass the *Basilica Aemilia, Tempio di Faustina, Tempio di Caesare* and *Arco di Augusto* and cross the Via Sacra to reach the *Rostra,* the platform for speakers; on the right are the *Lapis Niger,* the Black Stone above the grave of Romulus, the *Curia* of the senate and the *Arco di Settimo Severo;* on the left the *Tempio di Saturno* and *Basilica Julia,* the court building that Caesar had built shortly before he was killed, the rectangular *Tempio di Castore e Polluce* and the circular *Tempio di Vesta,* where the Vestals, maidens from the highest-ranking families, tended the sacred flame. Along the Via Sacra you pass the *House of the Vestals,* the *Tempio di Romolo,* which Maxentius built for a son who died young, and the *Basilica di Massenzio*, altered by Constantine.

At the entrance near the *Arco di Tito* a path leads up to Palatine Hill, where many rich Romans, among them Cicero and Catullus, possessed villas. You can walk back down to the forum through lovely 16th-century gardens, the Orti Farnesiani. *Daily 9am till one hour before dusk | entrances: Largo Romolo e Remo (Via dei Fori Imperiali), Via di S. Gregorio 30, Piazza S. Maria Nova (Arco di Tito) | admission 12 euros (includes Colosseo and Palatine, valid 2 days) | bus 85, 87, 117, 175*

⑩ FORO DI TRAIANO/MERCATI TRAIANI (143 F5) *(𝄞 F9)*

The 125-foot-high Trajan's Column, erected in AD 113, the centrepiece of the last and most magnificent of the imperial forums, now gleams pearly white again

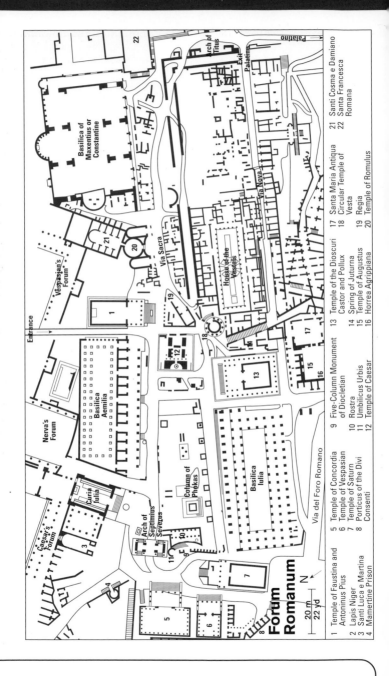

Forum Romanum

N

20 m
22 yd

Via del Foro Romano

1 Temple of Faustina and Antoninus Pius
2 Lapis Niger
3 Santi Luca e Martina
4 Mamertine Prison

5 Temple of Concordia
6 Temple of Vespasian
7 Temple of Saturn
8 Porticus of the Divi Consenti

9 Five-Column Monument of Diocletian
10 Rostra
11 Umbilicus Urbis
12 Temple of Caesar

13 Temple of the Dioscuri Castor and Pollux
14 Spring of Juturna
15 Temple of Augustus
16 Horrea Agrippiana

17 Santa Maria Antiqua
18 Circular Temple of Vesta
19 Regia
20 Temple of Romulus

21 Santi Cosma e Damiano
22 Santa Francesca Romana

Basilica of Maxentius or Constantine

Vespasian's Forum

Via Sacra

House of the Vestals

Via Nova

Palatino

Arch of Titus

Exit
Palatino

Entrance

Basilica Aemilia

Nerva's Forum

Caesar's Forum

Curia Iulia

Arch of Septimius Severus

Column of Phokas

Basilica Iulia

after almost ten years of restoration. You can admire the 200-metre sculptural frieze depicting Emperor Trajan's war against the Dacians from below. *Tue–Sun 9am until one hour before dusk | admission 6.50 euros, good view from outside | Via 4 di Novembre/Via dei Fori Imperiali | bus 40, 64, 70, 117, 170*

◼11 MONUMENTO NAZIONALE A VITTORIO EMANUELE II
(137 E–F5) (*F9*)

A striking construction on Piazza Venezia is a snow-white marble pile, the National Monument in honour of Victor Emmanuel II, the first king of Italy after the achievement of unification in 1870. The monument, disrespectfully dubbed the 'typewriter', 'wedding cake' or even 'false teeth' by the Romans, can now be visited from inside, as it houses a museum devoted to Italian unity. From the *Terrazza delle Quadrighe,* the highest terrace with its decorative bronze horses, and from the INSIDER**TIP** cafeteria on the roof you get a superb view of the Forum Romanum and the whole city centre. *Daily 9.30am–7.30pm | lift 7 euros | entrance from S. Maria in Coeli, Piazza Venezia | bus 30, 40, 85, 87, 119*

◼12 MUSEI CAPITOLINI ★
(137 E–F5–6) (*F9*)

The Capitoline Museums, opened on the Capitol in 1471 by Pope Sixtus IV, are the world's first public exhibitions. Two buildings designed by Michelangelo, the *Palazzo Nuovo* and *Palazzo dei Conservatori,* are home to unique works of art from antiquity, including the Capitoline Venus, the Dying Gaul and many busts of emperors and philosophers. The most spectacular exhibit is the INSIDER**TIP** original equestrian statue of Emperor Marcus Aurelius. Since 2005 it has been placed under a glass roof in

Trajan's Column: the emperor's story winds its way to the top

the *Giardino Romano*, a courtyard of the Palazzo dei Conservatori. A copy stands on the Capitol square.

Treat yourself to a break in the cafeteria of the roof garden (open to those not visiting the museum) for a stunning view of the city! *Tue–Sun 9am–8pm | admission 6.50 euros, with Centrale Montemartini 9.90 euros (valid 7 days), free on last Sun of the month, 1.5-hour guided tour in English 3 euros | Piazza del Campidoglio | bus 95, 117, 119, 160, 170, 638*

13 PALATINO (143 F2) (*∅ F10*)

The foundations of the Roman Empire were laid on this romantic green hill. It was the site of the hut of the shepherd Faustulus, who is said to have raised Remus and Romulus. Here Romulus received by augury the sign foretelling that he and not his brother Remus would be the ruler of Rome. From the time of Augustus, Roman emperors resided on the Palatine, witness the ruins of imperial villas such as the *Casa di Livia*, named after Augustus' wife, the *Domus Augustana* and the *Domus Flavia* in the pine grove. *Daily 9am till one hour before dusk | admission 11 euros (ticket for Foro Romano and Colosseo valid for 2 days) | Piazza del Colosseo | Metro B: Colosseo*

14 PALAZZO MASSIMO ALLE TERME (140 C5) (*∅ H8*)

The ancient sculptures on the ground floor convey an excellent impression of everyday life in ancient Rome. By contrast the INSIDER TIP turquoise-coloured dining room of Empress Livia and the delicate frescoes of the apartments illustrate the lifestyle of the ruling class. *Tue–Sun 9am–7.45pm | admission 7 euros (also for Palazzo Altemps, Terme di Diocleciano and Crypta Balbi, valid 3 days) | Largo di Villa Peretti 1 | Metro A, B: Termini*

15 SAN CLEMENTE (144 B2) (*∅ H10*)

This unique church with three historic storeys is truly a journey back through time. The golden mosaics of the chancel arch and the apse (12th century) of the medieval upper church are a gem. You then descend to the lower church (4th century), dedicated to Clement, the fourth pope (88–97), where fragments of frescoes depicting the life of the saint can still be made out. This columned basilica, which the Normans destroyed, lies in its turn above a building used for the cult of the Persian god of light Mithras, whom many Roman legionaries worshipped in bloody rituals associated with bulls.

One level below that are the remains of a townhouse from Caesar's period, and underneath that you can hear water flowing in the *cloaca massima,* the ancient drain by means of which the Etruscans dried out a swamp 2600 years ago – the prerequisite for building the Forum Romanum. *Mon–Sat 9am–12.30pm, 3.30–6pm | Via di S. Giovanni in Laterano | Metro B: Colosseo, bus 117*

which Christ is said to have ascended into the house of Pontius Pilate and which St Helena brought from Jerusalem to Rome in the 5th century. The *Sancta Sanctorum*

No two pairs of columns are alike: the cloister of San Giovanni in Laterano

▓ SAN GIOVANNI IN LATERANO
(144 C3) (*⑪ J10–11*)

The premier basilica of the Christian world, badly damaged in 1993 in a bomb attack, was restored very rapidly. Until the exile of the popes in Avignon (1305–77) this basilica, a gift of Emperor Constantine for Pope Sylvester (314–335), was the seat of the pontificate. The Baroque architects Domenico Fontana and Francesco Borromini cautiously modified the church, which is supported by columns and has double aisles. From the outside only the façade is visible, as the church is surrounded by the Lateran Palace, cloister and baptistry. Opposite are the Holy Steps *(Scala Santa),*

of 1590 at the end is a private chapel for the popes. *Daily 7am–6.30pm, baptistery 9am–1pm | Piazza S. Giovanni in Laterano | Metro A: S. Giovanni, bus 117, tram/bus 3*

▓ SAN PIETRO IN VINCOLI
(144 A1) (*⑪ G9*)

The chains with which St Peter is said to have been incarcerated in the Mamertine prison are kept below the high altar as a precious relic. The attraction for most visitors, however, is Michelangelo's powerful and magisterial figure of Moses (1516). *Mon–Sat 8am–12.30pm, 3–6pm, Sun 8.45–11.45am | Piazza S. Pietro in Vincoli | bus 117*

CLASSICAL ROME

In Santa Maria Maggiore holy mass has been celebrated every day since the 5th century

18 SANTA MARIA IN COSMEDIN
(143 E3) (*E10*)

Pope Adrian I donated this church in the 8th century to a Greek Byzantine congregation that fled to Rome in the face of persecution in the east. The name (*cosmedin,* Greek for 'ornament') derives from the opulent golden mosaics made in the 12th century by the *Cosmati*, a famous family of artists. In the sacristy is an icon of the *Theotokos,* the mother of god, and a mosaic of John VII, and in the atrium the *Bocca della Verità. Daily 9am–1pm, 3–6pm | Piazza Bocca della Verità | bus 30, 160*

19 SANTA MARIA MAGGIORE
(140 C6) (*H8*)

The patriarchal basilica on the Esquiline Hill is the largest of the 80 churches in Rome dedicated to the Virgin Mary, hence its name *maggiore*. Its campanile (1377) is the city's tallest. Behind the lively Rococo façade are treasures from the early Christian era. The golden mosaics in the nave and on the chancel arch as well as the floors with stone mosaics by the Cosmati family are among the finest in Rome. The coffered ceiling from the time of the Borgia pope Alexander VI (1492–1503) is covered in gold that Spanish conquerors robbed from the inhabitants of the newly discovered American continent.

Each year on the evening of 5 August flowers, scraps of paper or laser beams are used to create a white illusion on the Esquiline Hill that commemorates the founding of the church. On this evening in the year 352 the Virgin Mary is said to have instructed Pope Liberius to build a church in a place where he found snow. *Daily 7am–7pm | Piazza S. Maria Maggiore | bus 70, 71, 75*

20 SANTA PRASSEDE (144 B1) (*H9*)

It is just a few paces from the church of S. Maria Maggiore to this small basilica with outstanding 9th-century Byzantine mosaics on the chancel arch and in the apse. Legend tells that Prassede was converted to Christianity by St Peter. The *Cappella di S. Zenone,* which glows golden in the right-hand aisle, was regarded by pilgrims in the Middle Ages as a paradise garden. *Daily 7.30am–12 noon, 4.30–6.30pm | Via S. Prassede | bus 70, 71, 75*

⁂ STAZIONE TERMINI
(141 C–D 5–6) (*𝄞 H–J8*)

If you arrive by train it's worth looking up The light-flooded annexe that flows like a wave of glass and marble to Piazza dei Cinquecento was built in 1950 to designs by Luigi Nervi. *Metro A, B: Termini*

⁂ TERME DI DIOCLEZIANO
(140 C5) (*𝄞 H7*)

Opposite Stazione Termini lie the largest Roman baths, which today are part of the collection of antiquities of the *Museo Nazionale Romano.* Emperor Diocletian inaugurated this temple to hygiene and relaxation in AD 306 with an amazing 2400 water basins and baths. In the Baroque period a Carthusian monastery designed by Michelangelo and the church of *Santa Maria degli Angeli* were constructed over the ruins of the bath. In the *Chiostro di Michelangelo* thousands of inscriptions convey an idea of life in ancient times. *Admission 7 euros (also valid for Palazzo Altemps, Palazzo Massimo and Crypta Balbi) | Metro A, B: Termini, Piazza dei Cinquecento*

⁂ VILLA CELIMONTANA
(144 B3–4) (*𝄞 G11*)

The Hill of Caelius above the Colosseum is a veritable treasure trove for archaeologists. Above the Via Claudia are the remains of the Temple of Claudius. The Flavian Aqueduct runs through the mid-

dle of the park, and around the dilapidated villa of the Società Geografica are marble sculptures, columns and a half-hidden obelisk. There is a wonderful children's playground beneath the pine trees. *Via Claudia | bus 81, 117, tram 3*

SOUTHERN CENTRO STORICO

From Piazza Navona to the ghetto. The heart of the historic city, the 'Centro Storico' with its Renaissance and Baroque palaces, gushing fountains and crooked alleys, lies between Via del Corso, Piazza Venezia and the bend in the Tiber.

This is also the political epicentre of Italy. Piazza Colonna, where the Column of Marcus Aurelius tells of victories in battle against the Marcomanni, is the site of Palazzo Chigi, the seat of the prime minister. Behind it on Piazza Montecitorio is the national parliament, which has not seen its most glorious days in the era of Berlusconi. A walk through the narrow streets will almost automatically bring you to Piazza Navona, a Baroque arena for people-watching, and to Campo de' Fiori. In recent times not everything has been rosy in the heart of Rome. Exorbitant rents have driven out many of the old residents, and the ironsmiths and basket weavers can't keep their heads above water in the rising tide of fashion boutiques.

⁂ CAMPO DE' FIORI ★ ●
(136 C5) (*𝄞 D9*)

At the centre of this popular piazza stands a memorial to Giordano Bruno, a heretical Dominican monk who was burned at the stake here by the Inquisition at the start of the Holy Year of 1600. From beneath his hood Bruno looks defiantly towards the Vatican past the lively goings-on of the market in the mornings and the party people in the evenings. On Rome's favourite vegetable market fewer stands are to be found nowadays than in the past, as the competition from supermarkets takes its toll, but many Roman women still swear by the Campo, where lots of greens, root vegetables, spices and even clothes are on sale, though not many flowers despite the name of the square, which comes from a flower-covered meadow that was here in the Middle Ages. Situated between Corso Vittorio Emanuele and the high-class Piazza Farnese, and surrounded by tall restored palazzi, it is a romantic place to eat and a well-frequented rendezvous for fashionable Romans, especially in the evening, when the restaurants put out their tables. *Bus 40, 63, 64, 116*

▓ CRYPTA BALBI (137 D5) (*m E9*)

A pre-Christian Mithraeum – the cult of Mithras had many adherents in the Roman legions – and the remains of the *Teatro di Balbo* from the time of imperial Rome (13 BC) were uncovered in the vaults of a medieval townhouse. The visit gives you an excellent cross-section of Roman architectural history. *Tue–Sun 9am–7.45pm | admission 7 euros (includes Palazzo Massimo, Altemps and Terme di Diocleciano, ticket valid 3 days) | Via delle Botteghe Oscure 31 | bus 40, 46, 62, 64, 70, tram 8*

▓ FONTANA DELLE TARTARUGHE (137 D5) (*m E9*)

In 1584 Taddeo Landini made the much-loved Tortoise Fountain. Its bowl is coquettishly held by four slender boys. The INSIDER TIP bronze tortoises, which the boys are lifting to the rim of the bowl to let them drink, are said to have been added by Gianlorenzo Bernini when the

Campo de' Fiori: Rome's favourite square for market shopping and a meal in romantic surroundings

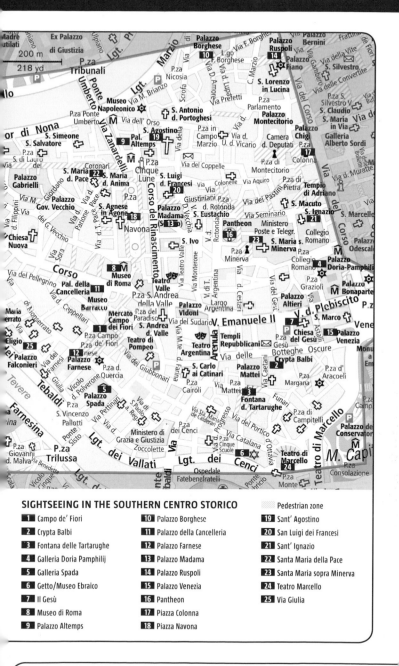

SIGHTSEEING IN THE SOUTHERN CENTRO STORICO

1 Campo de' Fiori
2 Crypta Balbi
3 Fontana delle Tartarughe
4 Galleria Doria Pamphilij
5 Galleria Spada
6 Getto/Museo Ebraico
7 Il Gesù
8 Museo di Roma
9 Palazzo Altemps

10 Palazzo Borghese
11 Palazzo della Cancelleria
12 Palazzo Farnese
13 Palazzo Madama
14 Palazzo Ruspoli
15 Palazzo Venezia
16 Pantheon
17 Piazza Colonna
18 Piazza Navona

19 Sant' Agostino
20 San Luigi dei Francesi
21 Sant' Ignazio
22 Santa Maria della Pace
23 Santa Maria sopra Minerva
24 Teatro Marcello
25 Via Giulia

Pedestrian zone

fountain was restored in 1658. *Piazza Mattei | bus 40, 62*

4 GALLERIA DORIA PAMPHILIJ
(137 E4) (*m E8*)

The Rococo façade of Palazzo Doria Pamphilij on Via del Corso has recently been renovated. Behind it, in a gallery decorated with gold and frescoes, artworks by Titian and Velazquez hang in rows, sometimes three paintings one above the other, on walls of silk wallpaper. This is one of Rome's most important private collections. *Fri–Wed 10am–5pm | admission 10 euros | Via del Corso 305 | www.doriapamphilj.it | bus 62, 63, 117, 119*

5 GALLERIA SPADA (136 C5) (*m D9*)

The palazzo of 1540 is itself a masterpiece of Italian Mannerism. Take a look at the INSIDER TIP play on perspective in the courtyard that Francesco Borromini designed for Cardinal Bernardino Spada. The statue of Mars seems to be large and some distance away from you, but the passageway is in reality only 9 metres long and the statue 1 metre high. The optical illusion was achieved by decreasing the size of the colonnade towards the back.

The upper floor is home to an excellent collection of paintings of the 17th and 18th centuries, with works by Annibale Carracci, Titian, Guido Reni, Domenichino and Caravaggio. *Tue–Sun 9am–7.30pm, in winter until 2pm | admission 5 euros | Piazza Capo di Ferro 3 | www.galleria borghese.it | bus 62, 64, 116*

6 GETTO/MUSEO EBRAICO
(137 D6) (*m E9*)

The ghetto, also called the *Villagio dei Ebrei*, lies between the Tiber, the Teatro di Marcello and the Portico d'Ottavia. The first Jews settled here as early as the 2nd century BC, which puts them among the true *romani romani*, the oldest citizens of Rome. Roman law granted them equality and religious freedom for centuries until the missionary zeal of the Christians made them a persecuted minority. In the Middle Ages and Baroque period they suffered under narrow-minded popes, who made them race against horses along Via del Corso as a popular amusement. In 1555 Pope Paul IV built a wall around the ghetto, and this confinement was not lifted until the time of the republic in 1870. The worst day in the ghetto, however, was 16 October 1943, when the Gestapo herded 2091 Jews onto trucks at the Portico d'Ottavia and deported them to death camps. Today about 400 Jewish families still live here. In the synagogue the new *Museo Ebraico* displays precious silver items and robes, and organises guided tours through the ghetto *(Sun–Thu 10am–5pm (June–Sept 10am–7pm), Fri 9am–2pm | admission 10 euros | Lungotevere Cenci | www.museo ebraico.roma.it)*. Bus 63

7 IL GESÙ (137 E4–5) (*m E9*)

Ignatius of Loyola, the Spanish founder of the 'Society of Jesus', commissioned the building of this Baroque construction, the Jesuits' main church, in 1568. Architect Vignola had an idea that was much imitated: placing a dome at the crossing of the nave and the transepts of a building originally like an early Christian hall church. *Piazza del Gesù | bus 40, 62, 63, 64, 70, 87*

8 MUSEO DI ROMA (136 C4) (*m D8*)

In a city that amounts to an archaeological park covering 3000 years, who needs a museum devoted to the last four or five centuries? However, following restoration work that seemed to last an eternity, *Palazzo Braschi* now houses exhibitions of wonderful Renaissance and Baroque works: frescoes and paintings from Roman palaces, engravings, terracottas, textiles, coaches, photos. *Tue–Sun 9am– 7pm | admission 6.50 euros | Via di San Pantaleo | www.museodiroma.it | bus 30, 40, 62, 64, 70, 116, 492*

Borghese (park) and Galleria Borghese (museum) – the nickname *cembalo,* as the short façade with two columned balconies facing the banks of the Tiber looks like a keyboard. Cardinal Camillo

The imposing architecture of Il Gesù was a model for many Baroque churches all over Europe

⑨ PALAZZO ALTEMPS
(136 C2) (*⑭ D8*)

Aphrodite, Apollo, Hermes and Ares: some years ago the divine ancient sculptures of the unique Ludovisi Collection moved into the lavishly refurbished Palazzo Altemps with its magnificent frescoes, just behind Piazza Navona. *Tue– Sun 9am–7.30pm | admission 7 euros (ticket includes Palazzo Massimo, Crypta Balbi and Terme di Diocleciano, valid for 3 days) | Piazza S. Appollinare 46 | bus 70, 81, 116, 492*

⑩ PALAZZO BORGHESE
(137 D1) (*⑭ E7*)

Its curious shape has earned the city residence of the aristocratic Borghese family – not to be confused with the Villa

Borghese, the later Pope Paul V (1605– 21), presented the palace to his brothers. Although the building today is used for public offices, you can still look inside the Baroque courtyard with its 96 columns, round arches and classical statues. *Piazza Borghese | Via Ripetta | bus 81, 117, 119*

⑪ PALAZZO DELLA CANCELLERIA
(136 B4) (*⑭ D8*)

The money to build this Renaissance palace, 60,000 scudi (about £700,000 in today's money) was won in 1483 by Cardinal Raffaele Riario when gambling with colleagues – nephews of the pope whose families were wealthy. Since 1870 it has been home to the Apostolic Chancellery with the *Sacra Romana Rota,* the papal court for marital matters, on extra-territorial land belonging to the Vatican. *Piazza della Cancelleria | bus 40, 62, 64, 116*

🔢 PALAZZO FARNESE
(136 B5) *(ⓜ D9)*

The elegant Palazzo Farnese near Campo de' Fiori is occupied by the French embassy. Usually, for security reasons, it is not even possible to sneak a glance inside the courtyard, which Michelangelo designed in 1546. If you are keen to see the beautiful gallery with famous frescoes by Annibale Carracci (1597–1604), join one of the guided tours organised by the cultural office of the French embassy *(tel. 06 68 60 11). Piazza Farnese | bus 116*

🔢 PALAZZO MADAMA
(136 C3) *(ⓜ D8)*

Pope Clement VII (1523–34) de' Medici pulled off the political feat of marrying off his illegitimate son Alessandro to the illegitimate daughter of Emperor Charles V, Margaret of Parma. 'Madama', as she was fondly called by the people of Rome, only lived in this Renaissance palace, where her husband was murdered, for a year. Since 1871 it has been the seat of the Italian senate. *Corso di Rinascimento | bus 70, 81, 87, 492*

🔢 PALAZZO RUSPOLI (137 D1) *(ⓜ E7)*

This fine Renaissance palace is now used for exhibitions of antiquities. *Sun–Fri 10am–7pm, Sat 10am–8.30pm | admission 6 euros | Via del Corso 418 | www.palazzoruspoli.it | Metro A: Spagna*

🔢 PALAZZO VENEZIA
(137 E4) *(ⓜ E–F9)*

For 200 years this fortress-like palace built in 1451 by Pope Paul II belonged to the Republic of Venice. It then fell into the hands of the Habsburgs, became the seat of government of Benito Mussolini and today houses a museum of applied art. *Piazza Venezia | bus 40, 63, 64, 117, 119*

🔢 PANTHEON ⭐ (137 D3–4) *(ⓜ E8)*

A cylinder with a dome on top: the Pantheon, built in 27 BC at the behest of Marcus Agrippa, the son-in-law of Augustus, to honour all the gods, is a brilliantly simple construction. Inside, the effects of light on sunny days are wonderful. Why does this ancient temple, which was rebuilt by Emperor Hadrian, desecrated in the Baroque and period and requisitioned as a memorial space for the Italian royal family, lie conveniently for tourists at ground level, when in the age of classical Rome it was entered by ascending five steps? In the course of time the city piled up six metres of rubble, and the architecture of antiquity sank beneath it all. *Mon–Sat 9am–7.30pm, Sun 9am–6pm | free admission | Piazza della Rotonda | bus 116*

🔢 PIAZZA COLONNA (137 E3) *(ⓜ E8)*

Not only Trajan's Column on Trajan's Forum has been restored. The Column of Marcus Aurelius on Piazza Colonna is also newly resplendent. Erected in AD 176 to honour Marcus Aurelius after his victory over the Marcomanni, it is covered with a frieze that represents a fine moral history of ancient times – for the edification of modern politicians too, as on the right stand Palazzo Chigi, seat of the prime minister, and behind it, on Piazza di Montecitorio, the Italian parliament meets in an elegant palace designed by Bernini that is shown every evening on the TV news. In case of demonstrations, an underground passage is available so that politicians can make a getaway. *Bus 63, 116, 119*

🔢 PIAZZA NAVONA ⭐ ●
(136 C3–4) *(ⓜ D8)*

The most beautiful and cheerful arena

of the Baroque period, elongated but enclosed, lively and colourful but at the same time intimate, is the work of Renaissance and Baroque popes, like so many of the attractive squares and streets in Rome. To please his beloved sister-in-law Olimpia, Innocent X (1644–55) not only ordered the construction of Palazzo Pamphili, today the seat of the Brazilian embassy, for her, but also spread this wonderful piazza at her feet. It was laid out on the site of the ancient games arena of Emperor Domitian (81–96), the *circo agonale*, out of which the people of Rome made the word *navona*. Until the late 18th century princes of the Church and patrician families enjoyed contests and horse races here from the windows of their palaces. To cool the Romans down in the summer hat, the piazza was flooded in August so that miniature naval battles could be staged. This Baroque arena is to this day a place of rendezvous for the residents of Rome, a superb stage for poor performers and wealthy show-offs, mediocre artists and street hawkers, well-known people about town and mongrels who trot to and fro past the ever-busy tables of the cafés.

Gianlorenzo Bernini's Fountain of Four Rivers, the *Fontana dei Quattro Fiumi*, is the undisputed centre of attention on the piazza. Four river gods are seated on a rocky grotto crowned by an obelisk. They represent the Danube, Nile, Ganges and Rio de la Plata. The last of these has taken up such a defensive posture that he seems to be afraid that the church of Sant'Agnese opposite is about to collapse – and indeed, the church was designed by Bernini's rival Francesco Borromini. This is, however, a myth, as the Baroque church was built two years after completion of the fountain. *Bus 40, 64, 70, 81, 116, 492*

A look behind the Pantheon's ancient temple front reveals a 43-metre rotunda

SOUTHERN CENTRO STORICO

19 SANT'AGOSTINO
(136 C2–3) (*D8*)

Behind this harmonious Renaissance façade, built of blocks of stone taken from the Colosseum, great art awaits, including the Madonna del Parto by Jacopo Sansovino (1521). From the third column of the nave Raphael's Prophet Isaiah ascends to heaven, and the first chapel on the left shelters Caravaggio's Madonna di Loreto (1605). *Daily 7.45–11am and 4–7.30pm | Piazza S. Agostino | bus 70, 81, 116, 492*

20 SAN LUIGI DEI FRANCESI
(136 C3) (*D8*)

The church of the French in Rome, dedicated to St Louis, was begun in 1518 but not finished until 1589 by Giacomo della Porta. In the fifth chapel on the left are INSIDER TIP three paintings by Caravaggio. *Daily 8.30am–12.30pm, Fri–Wed also 3.30–7pm | Piazza S. Luigi dei Francesi behind Palazzo Madama) | bus 70, 81, 87, 116, 492*

21 SANT'IGNAZIO (137 E3) (*E8*)

The geometrical Baroque façade forms a counterpoint to the adjoining elaborate Rococo buildings. Inside this Jesuit church, dedicated to the founder of the Jesuit order, Ignatius of Loyola, Andrea Pozzo created a masterpiece of the painter's art in 1685. The tall dome that visitors think they can see in the middle of the nave is in fact pure illusion. ● The church is often the venue for classical concerts. *Daily 7.30am–12.30pm, 3–7pm | Piazza S. Ignazio | bus 62, 116, 117, 119*

22 SANTA MARIA DELLA PACE
(136 B–C) (*D8*)

The façade alone is remarkable. The art-loving Pope Sixtus IV had an existing church near Piazza Navona rebuilt in 1482 in the Renaissance style. In 1656 the Baroque façade was added. Unfortunately the church of 'the Virgin of peace', in which Raphael painted famous figures of sibyls in the Cappella Chigi, has been almost permanently closed in recent years. The adjacent cloister by Donato Bramante now houses a cultural centre named INSIDER TIP *Chiostro del Bramante* with a café on the first floor *(Tue–Sun 10am–7.30pm | Arco della Pace 5, Via della Pace | bus 30, 40, 62, 64, 70, 116, 492*

23 SANTA MARIA SOPRA MINERVA
(137 D4) (*E8*)

The only Gothic church in Rome was built for the Dominican order in 1280 above the ruins of a temple dedicated to Minerva. To the left of the altar is Michelangelo's powerful figure (1521) of Christ holding the cross and the instruments of his martyrdom; the bronze loincloth was welded on at a later date. The *Cappella Caraffa* in the south transept holds famous frescoes by Filippo Lippi that tell the life story of St Thomas Aquinas (1492). In front of the church stands a small elephant by Bernini with a saddle that is much too big: 'Minerva's chick'. *Daily 8am–7pm | Piazza della Minerva | bus 117, 119*

24 TEATRO MARCELLO
(137 D–E6) (*E9*)

The Teatro Marcello became an archaeological park only recently and is now open day and night. Classical concerts are held in the ruins of this ancient theatre, which Julius Caesar began and Augustus completed. *Via del Teatro di Marcello 44 | bus 30, 44, 63, 95, 160, 170, 781*

25 VIA GIULIA
(136 A–B 3–5) (*C–D 8–9*)

Via Giulia is still a romantic street with fountains, gateways and flowering shrubs that overhang old walls. The Renaissance pope Julius II gave his architects freedom to design this noble row of buildings as they thought fit. Many of the palazzi here belonged to the Medici and other Florentine families. The court painter Raphael lived at no. 85 with a series of mistresses, the architect Antonio Sangallo occupied no. 66, and no. 93 was the residence of the man who later became Pope Paul III. *Bus 116*

NORTHERN CENTRO STORICO

From Piazza del Popolo to the Quirinal Palace: the fashion district between the Spanish Steps and Via del Corso is a great area for strolling past sights and shop windows.

When they occupy the walls of old Roman palazzi, the numerous boutiques of the world of *alta moda* ('high fashion') seem twice as elegant. Via del Corso used to be the shopping strip where young people bought their leather jackets and cheap glad-rags. Now new luxury boutiques like that of the five Fendi sisters or the Geox shoe salon extend an invitation to do some high-class shopping. The most exclusive streets are Via Condotti and Via del Babuino, and the cheapest is Via del Tritone.

When the retail experience has worn you out, let the spraying waters of the *Fontana di Trevi* refresh you or pay a call to the president of Italy in the *Quirinal Palace*. If he is not there to receive you, at least there's a good view from the piazza with the Dioscuri.

The ruins of the Teatro Marcello can hold concerts for audiences of up to 20,000

Richard Meier designed a modern shelter for the ancient Roman Altar of Peace, the Ara Pacis

1 ARA PACIS AUGUSTAE
(139 E4) (*∅ E7*)

An INSIDER TIP ultra-modern construction of steel and glass above Emperor Augustus' 2000-year-old Altar of Peace: this project by the American architect Richard Meier drew a barrage of criticism much like the reaction to the glass pyramid at the Louvre in Paris. But after ten years of complaints and protests, the people of Roman have mostly come to accept the structure. Opposite it is the *Mausoleo di Augusto, which was built in 27 BC. Tue–Sun 9am–7pm | admission 6.50 euros | Via di Ripetta | bus 70, 81, 117*

2 CASA DE CHIRICO
(137 E1) (*∅ E–F 6–7*)

It's as if he could return at any moment! After the death of the Surrealist painter Giorgio de Chirico, his bohemian apartment was converted to a museum. *Tue–Sat 10am–1pm by appointment only | tel. 0 66 79 65 46 | admission 5 euros | Piazza di Spagna 31 | Metro A: Spagna, bus 117*

3 CASA DI GOETHE (139 E4) (*∅ E6*)

'O, how happy I feel in Rome! To think of the time when a grey northern day was around', said the German poet and all-round genius, who spent 15 months in Rome in 1786–87. The apartment that he shared with his painter friend Heinrich W Tischbein is now a museum and cultural venue. *Tue–Sun 10am–6pm | admission 4 euros | Via del Corso 18 | www.casadi goethe.it | bus 117, 119*

4 FONTANA DEL TRITONE
(140 A5) (*∅ F7*)

High up on a shell-shaped bowl supported by four graceful dolphins, the triton blows a jet of water from his shell-like horn. Gianlorenzo Bernini made this fountain in 1637, and seven years later was also responsible for the second fountain on the piazza, the *Fontana delle Api*. On the latter, at the corner of Via Veneto and Via Basilio, water spurts from three bees, the heraldic beasts of the Barberini family – who brought forth a number of art-loving popes. *Piazza Barberini | Metro A: Barberini*

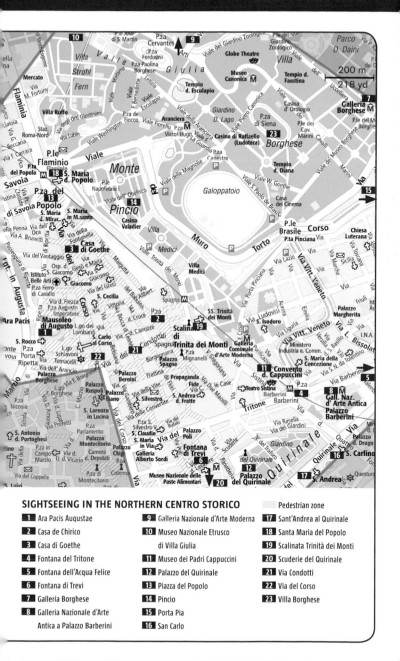

SIGHTSEEING IN THE NORTHERN CENTRO STORICO

░░░ Pedestrian zone

1 Ara Pacis Augustae
2 Casa de Chirico
3 Casa di Goethe
4 Fontana del Tritone
5 Fontana dell'Acqua Felice
6 Fontana di Trevi
7 Galleria Borghese
8 Galleria Nazionale d'Arte
Antica a Palazzo Barberini

9 Galleria Nazionale d'Arte Moderna
10 Museo Nazionale Etrusco
di Villa Giulia
11 Museo dei Padri Cappuccini
12 Palazzo del Quirinale
13 Piazza del Popolo
14 Pincio
15 Porta Pia
16 San Carlo

17 Sant'Andrea al Quirinale
18 Santa Maria del Popolo
19 Scalinata Trinità dei Monti
20 Scuderie del Quirinale
21 Via Condotti
22 Via del Corso
23 Villa Borghese

5 FONTANA DELL'ACQUA FELICE
(140 B5) (*ⓓ G7*)

A marble Moses gazes grimly from the triple arch out of which the water springs, but the four black lions at his feet have a more benign air. At night this fountain, the work Domenico Fontana completed in 1588, is especially atmospheric. *Piazza S. Bernardo | bus 60, 61*

6 FONTANA DI TREVI ★
(137 F3) (*ⓓ F8*)

Rome's largest and most popular fountain occupies a little square surrounded by six-storey palazzi. It was the last great monument of the Baroque popes, whose power was waning by 1750, the year of its construction. The god of the sea, Oceanus, rides through a triumphal arch with two horses. It's not only tourists hoping to come back to Rome some day who throw coins into the fountain. *Piazza di Trevi | bus 62, 63, 81, 85, 95, 116, 119, 492*

7 GALLERIA BORGHESE ★
(140 B2–3) (*ⓓ G5*)

Miracles happen, but in the Eternal City they sometimes take an eternity: after a 17-year restoration, the Baroque pleasure palace of Cardinal Scipione Borghese reopened. The prelate who promoted the career of the young Gianlorenzo Bernini was one of the world's great patrons of art. On the ground floor you can see Bernini's sculptures Daphne and Apollo, David and The Rape of Proserpina, as well as Antonio Canova's portrayal of Paolina Borghese, Napoleon's sister, in all her naked glory. Works by Lucas Cranach, Titian, Paul Veronese, Raphael, Peter Paul Rubens and Caravaggio hang on the first floor. *Tue–Sun 8.30am–7.30pm by prior appointment (in English too), tel. 0 68 41 39 79 | www.ticketeria. it | admission 8.50 euros | Piazza Scipi-one Borghese 5 | www.galleriaborghese. it | bus 52, 53, 116, 490, 495*

8 GALLERIA NAZIONALE D'ARTE ANTICA A PALAZZO BARBERINI
(140 B5) (*ⓓ G7*)

Some of the Titians and Tintorettos have to be kept in the cellar to allow army officers to dine in the Baroque halls: the Italian army uses much of Palazzo Barberini as an officers' mess. In the part that's a museum you can admire such masterpieces as Raphael's Fornarina, Caravaggio's Narcissus at the Spring and Hans Holbein's Henry VIII. Book in advance to visit the 18th-century rooms: *tel. 0 63 28 10 or www.ticketeria.it. Tue–Sun 9am–7pm | admission 5 euros | Via Quattro Fontane 13 | www.galleriaborghese.it | bus 62, 63, 116*

9 GALLERIA NAZIONALE D'ARTE MODERNA (139 F2) (*ⓓ E–F4*)

This gallery presents a good cross-section of 19th- and 20th-century art with works by Giorgio de Chirico, Gustav Klimt, Vincent van Gogh, Henry Moore, Picasso, Mondrian and Jackson Pollock. The well-stocked museum shop has an entertaining product range: *Libreria Gnam. Tue–Sun 9am–7.30pm | admission 10 euros | Viale delle Belle Arti 131 | www.gnam.arti. beniculturali.it | tram/bus 3, 19*

10 MUSEO NAZIONALE ETRUSCO DI VILLA GIULIA (139 E2) (*ⓓ E4*)

The summer residence constructed for Pope Julius III in 1550–55 has been dedicated since 1889 to the presentation of finds from Etruscan necropolises in Latium, Umbria and above all Tuscany: glass, jewellery, grave goods and sarcophaguses. In the garden you will find the reconstruction of a temple from Alatri. *Tue–Sun 8.30am–7.30pm | admission 8 euros | Piazzale di Villa Giulia 9 | tram/bus 3, 19*

Flanked by St Peter and St Paul, you pass through the Porta del Popolo to the Piazza del Popolo

ⅡⅠ MUSEO DEI PADRI CAPPUCCINI
(140 A5) (*ØJ F7*)

On Via Veneto a macabre but space-saving charnel-house admits visitors. Skull piled on skull, bone on bone: this is how Capuchin monks buried some 4000 of their brothers in tombs beneath *Santa Maria della Concezione* in centuries past. *Fri–Wed 9am–12 noon, 3–6pm | free admission | Via Veneto 27 | bus 58, 63, 116*

ⅡⅡ PALAZZO DEL QUIRINALE
(137 F7) (*ØJ F8*)

Pope Gregory XIII (1572–85) *desired a su*mmer residence that would be more comfortable, airy and modern than the Vatican. After the unification of Italy, this Renaissance palace became the seat of the Italian kings. Today it is the president of the republic who stretches his legs in the lovely Baroque gardens. A few state apartments and the park are accessible to visitors. *Sun 8.30am–12 noon, closed July–mid-Sept | admission 5 euros | Piazza del Quirinale | www.quirinale.it | bus 64, 70, 117, 170*

ⅠⅢ PIAZZA DEL POPOLO
(139 E3) (*ØJ E7*)

This spacious piazza was a kind of reception room for all travellers entering Rome from the Via Cassia or Via Flaminia. When Queen Christina of Sweden appeared at the gates in 1655, Bernini had just finished altering Michelangelo's Renaissance gateway. In 1830 Giuseppe Valadier created the neo-Classical steps and galleries that lead up to the Pincio. *Metro A: Flaminio, bus 117, 119*

ⅠⅣ INSIDERTIP PINCIO ☼
(139 E–F3) (*ØJ E6*)

To watch the sun go down from the Pincio Hill is part of the must-do programme for all lovers in Rome as well as for every tourist. Below lies Piazza del Popolo with the twin churches of *Santa Maria dei Miracoli* and *Santa Maria in Montesanto*, which look more interesting from the hill-top than they do from inside. In the distance you can make out the green strips bordering the river Tiber and the dome of *San Pietro. Metro A: Spagna or Flaminio*

15 PORTA PIA (140 C4) (*M H6*)

All schoolchildren in Italy know this city gate, a late work by Michelangelo, because it is where the soldiers fighting for Italian unity breached the city wall on 20 September 1870 and took possession of papal Rome: it was the founding hour of the Italian Republic, and the Pope withdrew ungraciously to the Vatican. Not until the signing of the Lateran Treaties in 1929 was the Pope recognised by the Italian state as the sovereign ruler of the Vatican. *Piazza Porta Pia | bus 60, 61, 62, 84, 90, 490, 495*

16 INSIDER TIP SAN CARLO (140 B5) (*M G8*)

Only a few steps away from Bernini's church of Sant'Andrea al Quirinale, his rival Borromini started work in 1638 on a Baroque gem with an oval dome on which he was to labour until his death in 1657. The concave and convex forms of the curving façade with its angel medallion are an architectural masterpiece. *Mon–Fri 9am–1pm, 3–5pm, Sat 10am–1pm, Sun 10.30am–1pm | Via del Quirinale/Via delle Quattro Fontane | bus 40, 64, 70, 117*

17 SANT'ANDREA AL QUIRINALE (140 A–B5) (*M G8*)

This Baroque church, a late work by Gianlorenzo Bernini dating from 1658–70 and now popular for weddings, seems like a salon in pink, gold and white with its unusual ground plan of a lateral oval.

Wed–Mon 9am–12 noon, 4–7pm | Via del Quirinale | bus 64, 65, 117

18 SANTA MARIA DEL POPOLO (139 E3) (*M E6*)

Just behind the Porta del Popolo is the Augustinian church in which Martin Luther celebrated mass in 1510 with other monks of his order. Inside, visitors are treated to an artistic feast: the frescoes in the choir and Cappella Rovere are by Pinturicchio; in the Cappella Cerasi, to the left of the altar, are the Conversion of St Paul and Crucifixion of St Peter by Caravaggio; the Cappella Chigi, the second from the right, was decorated by Raphael for a family of bankers; in the choir are two tombs by Andrea Sansovino; the marble figures of the high altar, on which is the Madonna del Popolo, are the work of Bernini and Lorenzetto. *Mon–Sat 7am–12 noon, 4–7pm, Sun 8am–1.30pm, 4.30–7.15pm | Piazza del Popolo | Metro A: Flaminio*

19 SCALINATA DI TRINITÀ DEI MONTI ★ ●
(137 E1) (*m E–F7*)

The curvy balustrades of the Spanish Steps below the French church *Trinità dei Monti* are the result of a conflict that lasted decades between the papacy and the French crown, as the French paid for the steps that lead up to their national church. In the end the popes forced through their own version and commissioned Alessandro Specchi and Francesco de Sanctis to build the steps in 1723. They take their English name from the open space below: Piazza di Spagna, and are as popular with young Romans as with tourists. It is forbidden to eat, drink and play the guitar there (prohibitions which are interpreted in true Italian style), but flirting is permitted.

Before the steps were constructed Pietro Bernini, a sculptor and father of the much more famous Gianlorenzo Bernini, created the *Fontana della Barcaccia,* a fountain in the form of a ship, which looks like a stranded Tiber barge in 1629. *Metro A: Spagna, bus 116, 117, 119*

20 SCUDERIE DEL QUIRINALE
(140 A6) (*m F8*)

Where once horses whinnied in the papal stables, you can now view major changing exhibitions such as the recent one on Caravaggio. INSIDER TIP ⟋ The view from the staircase is fantastic. *Opening times vary | Via XXIV Maggio 16 | www.scuderiequirinale.it | bus 60, 64, 70, 71, 117, 170*

21 VIA CONDOTTI (137 E1) (*m E7*)

Between the noisy Corso and the Spanish Steps runs Rome's most expensive and elegant shopping street. The streets parallel to it, Via Borgognona and Via Vittoria, are also filled with the very finest products of the fashion business. If

Possibly the most famous steps in the world: Scalinata di Trinità dei Monti, the Spanish Steps

The fashion street Via del Corso: only the northern section is free of traffic

you manage to keep your eyes on the citizens of Rome strolling here, you might be able to walk past the eye-wateringly expensive boutiques without financial damage. *Bus 117*

22 VIA DEL CORSO
(137 D–E 1–4) (ﾉﾉ E6–8)
The narrow Corso – today a popular shopping street – was once lined with palaces built by aristocrats. Today no horse-drawn coaches pass here, but great numbers of buses, taxis and government limousines, despite the closing of parts of the inner city to motorised traffic. Towards Piazza del Popolo traffic-calming measures are in place. *Bus 62, 63, 117, 119*

23 VILLA BORGHESE
(140 A–B 2–3) (ﾉﾉ F5)
In Rome's second-largest park you can relax after looking at the art in the *Galleria Borghese*, go inline skating or cycling, take a trip in a rickshaw or, in May,

attend the equestrian tournament on *Piazza di Siena*. At the north end of the park the INSIDER TIP former zoo is now an ecological park with many native animals, from frogs to a Roman wolf *(April–Oct daily 9.30am–7pm, Nov–March 9.30am–5pm | admission 12.50 euros)*. *Via Pinciana | bus 52, 53, 116, 490, 495, tram 19, 3*

PAPAL ROME

Vatican, Castel Sant'Angelo, Gianicolo. Rome and the papacy are indissolubly connected.

If you would like to get more than a fleeting impression of the Vatican with St Peter's Basilica, St Peter's Square, its art collections and the Castel Sant'Angelo, allow plenty of time. The Vatican Museums including the Sistine Chapel are not only home to the world's greatest collection of art treasures: in the tourist season they also have the longest queues.

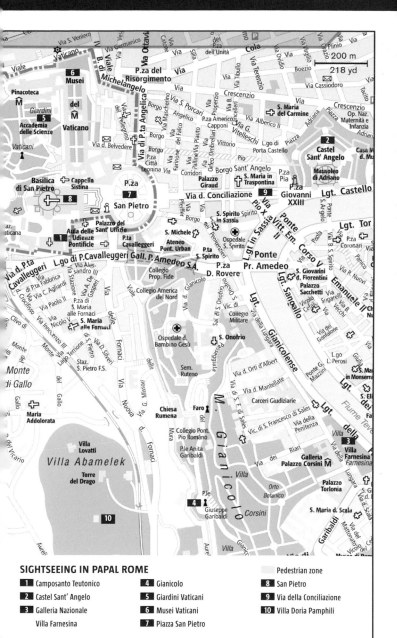

SIGHTSEEING IN PAPAL ROME

1 Camposanto Teutonico

2 Castel Sant' Angelo

3 Galleria Nazionale
Villa Farnesina

4 Gianicolo

5 Giardini Vaticani

6 Musei Vaticani

7 Piazza San Pietro

8 San Pietro

9 Via della Conciliazione

10 Villa Doria Pamphili

Pedestrian zone

From Castel Sant'Angelo the view ranges far and wide across the roofs of Rome

1 INSIDER TIP CAMPOSANTO TEU-
TONICO (138 A–B5) (*ɷ A8*)

This is a space of commemoration for the Germans in Rome. The entrance is behind the left-hand colonnade of San Pietro, and if you say the magic words 'Camposanto Teutonico', the Swiss Guard will let you through. The little cemetery in front of the Collegio Teutonico is the last resting place of the artist Stefan Andres, the archaeologist Ludwig Curtius and many German pilgrims who reached Rome and never returned home. *Mon–Sat 7am–12 noon | Piazza S. Pietro | bus 40, 64*

2 CASTEL SANT'ANGELO ☼
(136 A1–2) (*ɷ C7*)

This fortification, a place of refuge for the popes, was built above the cylindri-cal mausoleum of Emperor Hadrian (AD 117–138). It owes its name to a legend dating from Christmas in the year 590, when at the peak of a plague epidemic the Archangel Michael appeared to Pope Gregory I and sheathed his sword. With this gesture the plague ended. Since 1281 the castle has been connected to the Vatican Palace by a covered passage. Behind its strong walls are magnificent apartments for the popes, storerooms and some less-than-angelic torture chambers for heretics. From the battlements you get a fantastic view of Rome's most beautiful bridge, the *Ponte Sant'Angelo*, which leads across the Tiber to the city centre. Fortunately it is open only to pedestrians, so you can admire Bernini's ten Baroque angels in peace. *Tue–Sun 9am–7pm | admission 5 euros | bus 23, 40, 62*

3 GALLERIA NAZIONALE VILLA FARNESINA (136 A5) (*m C9*)

When Raphael painted his fresco of Amor and Psyche, the mistress of the owner of the house, the banker Chigi, is said to have been his model. The restored Renaissance architecture of Villa Farnesina, which Agostino Chigi commissioned from Baldassare Peruzzi in 1508, and the early use of perspective in the frescoes by Peruzzi are also worth taking in. *Mon–Sat 9am–1pm | admission 5 euros | Via della Lungara 230 | bus 23, 280*

4 GIANICOLO ☼ (142 B–C 1–2) (*m B–C 9–10*)

No high-rises and no TV tower spoil the view from the Gianicolo hill – dedicated to the two-faced god Janus – over the domes, churches and palaces of Rome. It is also the site of the equestrian statue of Italian freedom fighter Giuseppe Garibaldi, the hero of the unification of Italy. In 1849 he fought against French troops on this hill. *Bus 75, 115, 870*

5 GIARDINI VATICANI (138 A4–5) (*m A7*)

A large part of the Vatican state consists of the Vatican Gardens. In addition to monuments, green spaces and functional buildings they harbour the *Casina*, Pius IV's summer house of 1561, the papal Academy of Science and the Vatican radio station *(two-hour tours, pre-booking required at www.biglietteriamusei. vatican.va or in the Ufficio Visite Guidate | left-hand colonnade on St Peter's Square | tel. 06 69 88 46 76 | admission 30 euros, also valid for Musei Vaticani).*

Visits to the *Necropoli di Santa Rosa*, an ancient Roman burial ground that was recently discovered beneath the Vatican car park, are permitted only for groups who apply in writing to the *Ufficio Visite Speciali Giardini Vaticani (tel. 06 69 88 46 76 | visitespeciali.musei@ scv.va).*

6 MUSEI VATICANI (138 B4–5) (*m A–B 6–7*)

The Vatican Museums are the largest museum complex in the world, holding works of art in 1400 rooms. The range of exhibits Includes Egyptian mummies, Greek statuary, Roman mosaics, sarcophaguses, countless paintings, precious manuscripts (the *Biblioteca Apostolica* alone possesses 60,000 manuscripts, 7000 early printed works and some 800,000 prints), the most famous secret archive in existence, ethnographical rarities brought back by missionaries, the Pope's vehicles, including a Mercedes 600, and of course the Sistine Chapel, Raphael's Stanze and the Laocoön sculpture.

THE POPE ON THE WEB

When Pope Benedict XVI is in Rome, he holds a general audience on St Peter's Square on Wednesdays at 10am and says the Angelus prayer from the window of the Vatican Palace on Sundays at 12 noon *(www.vatican.va)*. Seats for papal audiences can be ordered by internet *(www.vatican.va | click on Info)*. For standing room at audiences on St Peter's Square you do not need a ticket, only pass the security checks. The Pope now has his own channel on *YouTube: www.youtube.com/vaticanit*.

The collections of the Vatican Museums include approximately 50,000 works of art

In the 20th century the collections were extended by adding the *Missionary Ethnological Museum* and the *Collezione d'Arte Religiosa Moderna,* founded in 1973 by Pope Paul VI. It contains works by Marc Chagall, Paul Klee, Vassily Kandinsky and Giorgio de Chirico, among other artists.

There is a single route through the 14 museums with their 50,000 exhibits, and it is 4.5 miles long. If you aim to actually enjoy this cultural marathon, there are two options: you come several times, or you set priorities and leave some things out, choosing one of the shorter circuits – though all routes finish up by passing through Raphael's Stanze and the Sistine Chapel, and all of them are one-way, a measure that is intended to channel around four million visitors per year through the collections without everything coming to a standstill.

INSIDER TIP Note: the entrance to the Musei Vaticani is in Viale Vaticano *(north side of the Vatican site, 10 min on foot from St Peter's Square). Mon–Sat 9am–6pm, last admission 4pm | admission 15 euros, last Sun of the month 9am–2pm free, last admission 12.30pm, ticket purchase by internet costs 4 euros extra, but it gets you inside* INSIDER TIP *when you want without the usual queuing; guided tours (available in English) 31 euros | www.vatican.va, www.christusrex. org | Metro A: Cipro-Musei Vaticani, bus 23, 32, 81*

APPARTAMENTO BORGIA

Pinturicchio painted the apartments (1492–95) of Alexander VI, a pope from the Borgia family. Cesare Borgia, the son of this pope, is said to have murdered his brother-in-law Alfonso of Aragon here in 1500.

CAPPELLA SISTINA ⭐

‚It's like the first moon landing,' the head restorer of the Sistine Chapel, Fabrizio Mancinelli, prophesied: ‚Afterwards the art world will be different.' And indeed, a completely new Michelangelo emerged from the last restoration of this artistic holy of holies. Once layers of dust and soot from candles had been removed, the robes of the figures from the story of creation on the ceiling of the papal domestic chapel glowed in shades of lime green, bright purple and orange. The great Renaissance painter – also known as *Il Divino* – was revealed as a Mannerist in the colours of Pop Art. It turned the art world on its head.

In the years 1508–12 Michelangelo Buonarroti (1475–1564) painted the whole, 41-metre-long ceiling all on his own using the fresco technique – not lying on his back, as the legend reports, but above his head, with a candle on his hat. 'I haven't got a good eye. I'm not cut out for painting,' wrote the sculptor Michelangelo to a friend.

What an understatement! With astonishing effects of depth, the maestro painted a story of Creation that will remain unique, from the creation of Adam and Eve, their sin and the Flood to the drunkenness of Noah. Of the 340 biblical scenes, the creation of Adam, on which the divine spark passes from hand to hand, is the most impressive and certainly the most often reproduced. Delicate sibyls and grim-looking prophets frame the fresco.

More than 20 years later, when Michelangelo was 60 years old, Pope Paul III commissioned him to paint the Last Judgement on the end wall of the chapel. When the finished work was unveiled at Christmas 1541, it caused a scandal: a naked Christ was revealed, gathering about him with a regal gesture a whirl of equally naked saints, the chosen, the resurrected and the damned – Michelangelo's superb final flourish.

Rome was on the threshold of the Counter-Reformation, and modern art lovers can count themselves lucky that the pious counter-reformers did not destroy the work immediately. However, Michelangelo's pupil Daniele de Volterra was obliged to paint some drapery around the loins of the naked figures. Some 460 years later, when The Last Judgement was restored, there was no scandal, but only applause. The Vatican trod a diplomatic path in the thorny question of the added drapery. The restorers were allowed to wash off 17 of the 40 loincloths. Honour was satisfied for Michelangelo, *Il Divino,* who painted a portrait of himself in the flayed skin of St Bartholomew.

MUSEO CHIARAMONTI

In the early 19th century the sculptor Antonio Canova was commissioned by Pope Pius VII, Barnaba Chiaramonti (1800–25), to furnish this passage with about 1000 sculptures of antiquity: it is a walk past statues and heads of Augustus, Caesar, Titus, Trajan, Demosthenes, Athene and a sculpture representing The Nile and His 16 Children, the recumbent river god personified with the branches of his delta.

MUSEO GREGORIANO EGIZIO

The papal Egyptian museum presents mummies and statues that were excavated in Egypt over the course of the 19th and 20th centuries or brought there from Villa Hadrian in Tivoli. Emperor Hadrian (AD 117–138) was a great lover of Egypt.

MUSEO PIO CLEMENTINO

In 1506 Pope Julius II sent his court sculptor Michelangelo personally to the Domus Aurea to inspect the Laocoön sculpture (2nd century BC), which had been found in rubble. This was the beginning of the world's most extensive collection of works from antiquity, original Greek and Roman works of the highest quality. In the *Cortile del Belvedere* (Belvedere Court) are the Apollo Belvedere (4th century BC) and the Laocoön group (2nd century BC), found in 1506. Michelangelo lavished praise on the 'Belvedere torso' in the *Atrio del Torso*. A further famous piece here is a Roman copy of the Venus of Praxiteles (4th century BC).

PINACOTECA

First-class paintings and sculptures from the Middle Ages to the late 19th century are shown in chronological order in 18 rooms: works by, for example, Giotto, Fra Angelico, Filippo Lippi, Lucas Cranach, Perugino, Raphael, Leonardo da Vinci, Pietro da Cortona, Titian, Paolo Veronese, Caravaggio, Anthony van Dyck and Gianlorenzo Bernini.

STANZE E LOGGE DI RAFFAELLO

Four rooms that Raphael painted for Pope Julius II, the so-called *Stanze,* and the attached *Loggie,* are among the greatest achievements of Italian Renaissance painting. The glowing colours of Raphael's fresco of The School of Athens – at its centre the philosophers Plato and Aristotle with a background of imposing Renaissance architecture – and his dramatic Fire in the Borgo have been freshly restored. Raphael painted the twelve ar-

cades of the *Loggie* with antique-style bands of grotesque figures and scenes from the Old Testament; only one fresco is devoted to the New Testament.

▮7▮ PIAZZA SAN PIETRO
(138 B5) (*Ⓜ B7*)

St Peter's Square, completed in 1667, is a masterpiece – and a tour de force of optical illusions. What seems to be a circular space is in fact an ellipse, and the flat-looking rectangle in front of the basilica is a trapezium that rises by four metres. Seen from the little marble slabs to the left and right of the fountain, the four rows of columns merge to a single colonnade. The semi-circular colonnades, adorned with statues of 140 saints, are like outstretched, welcoming arms. By such means the Baroque architect Gianlorenzo Bernini achieved his aim of bringing Michelangelo's perfect dome, which almost disappeared behind the ill-proportioned church façade by Carlo Maderno, back onto centre stage. Berni-

ni was aware of this, promising: 'You shall only speak of me in terms of great works.' *Bus 40, 46, 64, 98*

8 SAN PIETRO ⭐
(138 B5) (*∭ A–B7*)

St Peter's Basilica can only be described with superlatives. In size it far exceeds any other European church, measuring 211 m in length (a good 40 m longer than St Paul's Cathedral in London), 186 m at its widest point and 132 m in height. It can hold 60,000 worshippers. In 1506 Pope Julius II gave Donato Bramante the task of building a new church to replace the ancient basilica that Emperor Constantine erected over the tomb of St Peter. In the 120-year period of construction, the best architects in Italy came up with many mutually contradictory models: Bramante wanted a ground plan of a Greek cross (i.e. four equally long arms) with a massive dome, but to meet the wishes of later popes this was changed to a cross with one longer arm. The nave had not been completed when Michelangelo took up Bramante's ideas again in 1546 and started construction of a large dome on the model of the cathedral in Florence. Pope Paul V in his turn wanted St Peter's to have the longest nave of any Christian church and awarded Carlo Maderno the commission to extend it and build the façade, which however obstructed the view of the dome.

Inside the church on the right you stand in front of the Porta Santa, the Holy Door, which is opened only in a Holy Year. Michelangelo's Pietà is protected by bullet-proof glass in the first chapel on the right, as in 1972 a disturbed young man smashed its nose. On the pillar dedicated to St Longinius, the foot of a bronze statue of St Peter has been polished to a shine by the kisses of pilgrims. Marble steps in front of the papal altar lead down to the tomb of St Peter and the last resting place of Pope John Paul II. Above them stands the bronze baldachin designed by Bernini. The crowds of visi-

It's rarely as quiet as this on Piazza San Pietro, and certainly not when the Pope holds a general audience here

Deacons at the All Saints liturgy in San Pietro, the most important Christian basilica

tors have made it necessary to move the entrance to the papal tombs and the Vatican catacombs to the right-hand aisle. Two further works by Bernini are in the apse: the cathedra altar with the papal throne and the tomb of Urban VIII, a pope from the Barberini family. On the left in the nave is the entrance to the sacristy and the Vatican treasury.

To get up to the roof you take a lift to the right of the church. After that 320 steep steps lead up to the ☀ *dome,* from where the view of Rome is superb. A visit to the necropolis under the basilica has to be applied for in writing at the *Uffici Scavi (scavi@fsp.va | 12 euros). Church daily 7am–7pm, in winter until 6pm, sacristy 9am–6pm, in winter until 2.30pm | admission 2.50 euros; roof and dome 9am–6pm, admission 5 euros, with lift 7 euros, security checks beneath the right-hand colonnade; be sure to wear decent clothing, i.e. long trousers, no uncovered shoulders! | Metro A: Ottaviano, bus 40, 62, 64*

9 VIA DELLA CONCILIAZIONE

(138 C5) (*🕮 B–C7*)

In past times, after making their way through the little streets of Borgo Pio, pilgrims were suddenly confronted with the sight of the venerable St Peter's Square. In 1937 Benito Mussolini drove a broad thoroughfare through the borgo and fulfilled an old wish of the popes to have a showcase avenue leading up from the Tiber. The 'Road of Reconciliation' commemorates the conclusion of the Lateran Treaties of 1929, which sealed a settlement between the Vatican and the united Italian state. *Bus 23, 40, 62*

10 VILLA DORIA PAMPHILI
(142 A1–4) (*∅ A–B 9–11*)

Rome was cut in two in 1960 by the Via Olimpia, a connecting road built in a hurry for the Olympic Games. On the site where Caesar had a villa built for Cleopatra, Camillo Pamphili, a nephew of Pope Innocent X, built himself a palace in the Palladian style in 1644. Today it is used for official events. *Entrances: Via di S. Pancrazio, Via Aurelia Antica, Via Vitelia | bus 44, 870*

TRASTEVERE & TESTACCIO

Trastevere, Rome's largest village trans tiberim – i.e. across the Tiber, as it was called in Augustus' day – still has charm, even though in recent years it has perhaps been prettified too much.

Where once washing lines hung across the street and the old folk put their chairs on the pavement in the evening for a chat, an upmarket quarter for clubbing has emerged, especially for a foreign clientele. Neighbouring *Testaccio* too, once extremely quiet, has a lively nightlife now that bars and clubs have opened in the former slaughterhouse. However, in these districts there are still many residents who would not at any price sell their little apartments full of nooks and crannies. And those who have moved out come back each July for the *Festa de Noiantri*.

1 CIMITERO PROTESTANTE
(143 E5) (*∅ E12–13*)

This romantic cemetery overgrown with cypresses behind the Pyramid of Cestius was used for burials of Anglicans and other Protestants. INSIDER TIP Here are the graves of the English poets Keats, who died in Rome and Shelley, who drowned off the Italian coast, as well as Germans such as Goethe's son August and the architect Gottfried Semper, and the Marxist political philosopher Antonio Gramsci. *Mon–Sat 9am–5pm, Sun 9am–1pm | Via Caio Cestio | Metro B: Piramide, bus 60, 75, 118, 715, tram/bus 3*

2 MONTE TESTACCIO ⁂
(143 D5) (*∅ D–E 12–13*)

The 120-foot-high Testaccio hill consists of ceramic shards that are thousands of years old. This was the site of the wholesale market halls of ancient Rome. The traders sold their wares in amphorae, large pottery jars, and disposed of them on this great historic tip. By booking one or two weeks in advance, you can take part in a guided tour given by the monument protection authority. *Via Galvani/Via Zabaglia | booking (Italian and English) info@zetema.it | tel. 06 06 08 | Metro B: Piramide, bus 60, 95, 673*

3 PIAZZA DEI CAVALIERI DI MALTA
(143 E4) (*∅ E11*)

A spot for romantics and key-hole peepers on the Aventine hill. In 1766 the architect and engraver Giovanni B. Piranesi built the seat of the Order of Knights of St John, which describes itself as a sovereign state and has its own car number plates, though it lacks its own territory. Look through the iron-bound keyhole of the wooden green gate of no. 4, the ● *Buco di Roma* – and you will get a surprising view of St Peter's Basilica in the distance. Piranesi also designed the square lined with palms and cypresses, a favourite rendezvous for lovers. *Metro B: Circo Massimo, bus 23, 30, 60, 75, 118, 175 tram*

4 PIRAMIDE DI CESTIO
(143 E5) (*Ø E12*)

In ancient times Egypt with its pyramids and obelisks was highly fashionable. That is why the praetor and tribune Caius Cestius had himself buried like a little pharaoh in a luxury pyramid tomb in 11 BC. *Piazza Ostiense | Metro B: Piramide, tram 3*

5 SAN PIETRO IN MONTORIO
(142 C2–3) (*Ø C10*)

According to a legend this church stands on the site where St Peter was crucified, but the attraction for most visitors is the unique *Tempietto* by Bramante, a Renaissance masterpiece in miniature format in the courtyard of the adjacent Franciscan monastery. This circular building surrounded by columns is well liked as a venue for weddings, hidden away from public view. *Piazza S. Pietro in Montorio 2 | bus 44, 115, 125*

6 SANTA CECILIA (143 E3) (*Ø E10*)

This small church with a Romanesque tower is dedicated to St Cecilia, a young martyr who is said to have sung gaily throughout the three days when she was tortured by the emperor's soldiers. This has earned her the role of patron saint of music. The marble statue of the fragile-looking saint below the altar was made in 1600 by Stefano Maderna. The 13th-century frescoes in the cloister are Pietro Cavallini's depiction of the Last Judgement *(Mon–Sat 10am–3pm, Sun 11.30am–12.30pm | admission 2.50 euros)*. From the crypt there is access to the Roman house in which Cecilia is said to have lived *(daily 9.30am–12.30pm, 4–6.30pm | admission 2 euros)*. *Piazza S. Cecilia 22 | tram 8*

7 SANTA MARIA IN TRASTEVERE
(142 143 C–D2) (*Ø D10*)

Behind an octagonal fountain, a gold mosaic of Mary and the Ten Holy Women (12th century) gleams on the façade of the oldest church in Rome dedicated to the Virgin Mary, dating from the 3rd century. The most beautiful mosaics are in the apse: Jesus larger than life-size with the Virgin and saints. *Daily 7am–8pm | Piazza S. Maria in Trastevere | bus H, tram 8*

8 TEVERE & ISOLA TIBERINA
(137 D6) (*Ø E10*)

In antiquity the island in the river Tiber was dedicated to Aesculapius, the god of healing. Around the year 1000 the Holy Roman Emperor Otto III built the church of San Bartolomeo on the remains of a temple. A church-run hospital *Fatebenefratelli* keeps up the medical tradition

A pyramid for a tomb: the Piramide di Cestio

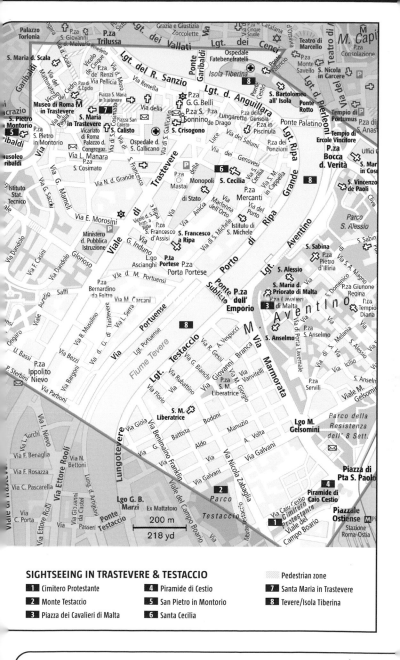

SIGHTSEEING IN TRASTEVERE & TESTACCIO

Pedestrian zone

1 Cimitero Protestante
2 Monte Testaccio
3 Piazza dei Cavalieri di Malta
4 Piramide di Cestio
5 San Pietro in Montorio
6 Santa Cecilia
7 Santa Maria in Trastevere
8 Tevere/Isola Tiberina

to this day. To reach the island, cross the *Ponte Fabrizio* and *Ponte Cestio*, the oldest and most beautiful of the 21 bridges across the Tiber. The Tiber was fully navigable until the 19th century. In the 1920s canoe clubs and public baths sprang up here. Today you can bask in the sun on a man-made beach or, if the water level is high enough, between April and October take a trip to St Peter's on the INSIDER TIP *Acquabus* (stops at Ponte Sant'Angelo). The two-hour *dinner cruise* with a three-course menu costs 58 euros. The *short cruise* with wine and cheese snacks *(only Fri/Sat/Sun 9pm)* costs 39 euros, the *hop-on hop-off trip* 15 euros. *Reservations tel. 06 97 74 54 98 | from Ponte Sant'Angelo, timetable varies depending on water levels | www.batelli diroma.it*

OUTSIDE THE CENTRE

CAMPO VERANO
(141 F5–6) (*M L–M 7–8*)
With lots of marble structures and plaster angels, this showy necropolis could be said to have a lively atmosphere, especially on All Saints' Day, when the people of Rome go to the graves of their deceased relatives to bring them flowers and wine in a bizarre combination of pomp, picnic and reverence for the dead. *Daily 9am–6pm | Piazzale S. Lorenzo fuori le Mura | tram/bus 19, 3*

CENTRALE MONTEMARTINI ★
(0) (*M E14*)
A radiant white Venus, the Aphrodite of Knidos, Roman emperors, generals and philosophers in a former power station? Don't miss this unusual stage for heroes and gods. *Tue–Sun 9.30am–7pm | admis-* sion 4.50 euros, combined ticket with Musei Capitolini 10.50 euros | Via Ostiense 106 | Metro B: Piramide or Garbatella, bus 716, tram/bus 3*

COPPEDÈ QUARTER
(140 C–D2) (*M H4*)
Not far from Piazza Buenos Aires a gateway opens to a stone-built land of fairytales. This is the strange realm of Gino Coppedè (1886–1924), architect of the 'Liberty style', INSIDER TIP with Art Nouveau palazzi and palatial buildings adorned with figures of fairies, spiderlike and fabulous beasts, Babylonian lions' heads and monsters. On *Piazza Mincio* stands a decorative frog fountain surrounded by dainty *Villini delle fate*, the fairies' houses. *Tram 3, 19, bus 63*

DIVES IN MISERICORDIA (0) (*M O*)
A must-see for all architecture fans: Richard Meier's new steel-and-concrete church in the eastern quarter of *Tor Tre Teste*, approx. six miles from the centre. *Daily 7.30am–12.30pm, 3.30–7.30pm | Via Tovaglieri | www.diopadremisericordioso.it | Stazione Termini bus 14 to Togliatti/Abele, then bus 556*

EUR – ESPOSIZIONE UNIVERSALE DI ROMA (147 D5) (*M O*)
For the World Exhibition of 1942, which did not take place on account of the Second World War, Benito Mussolini had this futuristic quarter built halfway between Rome and Ostia. From afar you can see the cuboid INSIDER TIP *Palazzo della Civiltà del Lavoro* with its 216 window niches. The dome of the *Palazzo dei Congressi* can be counted as an aesthetic example of Fascist architecture, as can the *Museo della Civiltà Romana*, which houses no original works but many excellent copies. The ● *Piscina delle Rose*, Rome's Olympic pool with a length of 50 m, a gym and a

Contrasts in the Centrale Montemartini: antique sculptures displayed in a power station

spa is also situated here *(Viale America 20 | www.piscinadellerose.it) | Metro B: EUR Marconi, then bus 30, 170*

PIGNETO (145 E–F 2–5) *(𝄂 M10)*
The suburb of Pigneto has retained the quirky charm of the 1950s. The author Carolina Cuttolo has described the quarter where she lives as a cross between 'Dolce Vita and the Bronx'. Jammed in between two arterial roads, Via Prenestina and Via Casilina, this district originally built for railway workers is an area of rented flats, little houses and allotment gardens. Around the main road of the quarter, Via del Pigneto, designers' shops, pubs and literary *enoteche,* cafés with books and wine, have sprung up, as Pigneto has attracted lots of creative people, musicians, gallery owners, designers and young film makers who can no longer afford the high rents in the Centro Storico. The film director Pier Paolo Pasolini found the right milieu of pimps and small-time criminals for Accatone in the bar *Necci dal 1924 (Via Fanfulla da Lodi 68)*. No other quarter has so many trendy film clubs, such as *Grauco (Via Perugia 34)* and *Cineclub Alphaville (Via del Pigneto 283)*. The *Nuovo Cinema Aquila* in Via Ascoli Piceno belonged to the Magliana band of gangsters, a fact that fits the area as much as the little mosque, as many Africans, Indians and Bangladeshis have settled in this peaceful multicultural quarter. And nature lovers can take a leafy walk beneath a 2000-year-old aqueduct, the *Acqua Claudia*. A plaster-cast studio with Roman busts and knick-knacks has been set up between the ancient arches. The heads of Caesars here are guarded by two sheepdogs – and a grunting pig. *Tram 5, 14, 19*

MAXXI ★ ● (0) *(𝄂 C2)*
It will take some while for the shock waves triggered by Zaha Hadid's mu-

seum for 21st-century art to die down – for both its admirers and its critics. The *Museo Nazionale delle Arti del XXI. Secolo* near the Stadio Flaminio, known by the short and sweet name MAXXI, is an exhibit in itself. Everything appears to be in motion in this building. Ramps suddenly seem to change places as if in a cartoon film, stairs lead up to heaven, and leaning walls or crooked corners tempt visitors to tread new artistic paths at every turn. The collection contains works by such artists as Francesco Clemente, Mario Merz and Gerhard Richter. *Tue–Sun 11am–7pm, Thu and Sat until 10pm | admission 11 euros | Via Guido Reni 2 | www.fondazionemaxxi.it | tram 2, bus 53, 280, 910*

MURA AURELIANE/PORTA SAN SEBSTIANO ☇ (144 C6) (*ᗐ H13*)

The twelve-mile fortification that encircled ancient Rome, the Aurelian Wall, is almost entirely preserved. In AD 271 Emperor Aurelian had it constructed in a hurry, fearing an invasion of Goths: 8 metres high, 18 main gates, 381 watchtowers – and 116 toilets. *Museo delle Mura, Tue–Sun 9am–7pm | admission 2.60 euros | Via Porta S. Sebastiano 18 | bus 218, Archeobus from Stazione Termini (Piazza Cinquecento) | fare 10–15 euros*

PONTE MILVIO (146 C4) (*ᗐ C1*)

In AD 312 Emperor Constantine defeated his main rival Maxentius at the Milvian Bridge. Charlemagne, Martin Luther, Holy Roman Fmperor Frederick II and Queen Christina of Sweden all passed over this historic bridge, but nowadays it belongs to lovers from all over the world. All INSIDER TIP▶ ten lampposts on the bridge have been covered with padlocks by couples who then throw the keys into the river Tiber as a symbolic act.

SAN PAOLO FUORI LE MURA (147 D4) (*ᗐ E16*)

In a fire of 1823 this patriarchal basilica, which lies outside the city wall (that's what the name means) was destroyed, with the exception of the mosaics on the chancel arch and ciborium above the altar. The neo-Classical church with its 14th-century cloister is visited by many pilgrims. *Daily 7.30am–12 noon, 4–8pm, in winter 7.30am–12 noon, 3.30–7pm | Via Ostiense 190 | Metro B: S. Paolo, bus 23, 128, 271, 761*

TERME DI CARACALLA (144 B4–5) (*ᗐ G12*)

In AD 537 the Goths destroyed the luxurious Baths of Caracalla, which had been built 300 years earlier by Emperor Caracalla and accommodated 1500 bathers. In summer performances of the *Teatro dell'Opera* are held here. *Tue–Sun 9am until one hour before dusk | admission 6 euros | Via delle Terme di Caracalla | Metro B: Circo Massimo, bus 118, 160, 714*

VILLA TORLONIA (141 E2–3) (*ᗐ K5*)

For decades Villa Torlonia had all the charm of a bombsite, as almost nothing remained of the neo-Classical splendour of the princes of Torlonia. Perhaps the ghost of the Fascist dictator Mussolini, who occupied the park and its magnificent buildings from 1925 to 1943, stalked the site. Since 1997 however the park has had a renaissance: step-by-step the grand architecture and the sequestered owl house *(Casina delle Civette)* have been restored and converted to museums for changing exhibitions. In the orangery, where the scent of lemons and oranges once filled the air, *La Limonaia* now serves simple Mediterranean cuisine. *Daily 9am–7pm | Via Nomentata 70 | bus 36*

TRIPS

CASTELLI ROMANI (147 E5–6) (*Ⅲ O*)

The pretty towns and villages in the region known by the Romans as *castelli romani* are situated on what must be the world's oldest wine route. Caesar and Brutus had villas in *Frascati* (approx. 12 miles south of Rome) in the Alban Hills. The Baroque residence of Cardinal Aldobrandini is not open to visitors, but you can see its park and *Teatro dell'Acqua*. What attracts most daytrippers is the delicious white Frascati wine to go with suckling pig, *porchetta,* eaten at a market stall. *Zaraza* is a popular place to eat and drink on the panoramic route *(closed Mon, and Sun evening in winter | Viale Regina Margherita 45 | tel. 06942 2053 | Moderate)*.

On the ☙ route to Castel Gandolfo you have a wonderful view of a volcanic lake, *Lago di Nemi,* where there are paths for walkers. The best-known resident of Castel Gandolfo is Pope Benedict XVI. Old Fabiola Moroni sends cakes to his palace as a greeting and leaving present, but she herself is modest: at her *Hosteria la Fraschetta (closed Mon | Via della Repubblica 58 | tel. 06936 13 12 | budget)* you can still get home-made pasta, for example *fettuccine* with ceps, for a mere 8 euros! *Directions: from the orbital motorway Grande Raccordo Anulare (G.R.A.), motorway A1 or N215 to Frascati or N7 to Castel Gandolfo; by train: from Termini to Frascati or Castel Gandolfo; bus: between Frascati and Castel Gandolfo blue Cotral buses run about every 30 min.*

CERVETERI (146 A3) (*Ⅲ O*)

At a time when Rome was little more than a village, the Etruscan city of *Caere,* now Cerveteri (28 miles north-west of Rome) was one of the largest in the Mediterranean region with 100,000 inhabitants. The Etruscan necropolises are a little bit outside the centre. The activities of *tombaroli*, grave robbers, fortunately spared the *Tomba degli Alari,* the grave of a woman that was discov-

Equally attractive for sun worshippers, fans of ruins and opera lovers: the Terme di Caracalla

ered in 1905 with a full set of household goods, jewellery and bottles of perfume. Of the eight graves in the *Necropoli di Banditaccia* that are open to visitors, the *Tomba dei Rilievi,* the 'tomb of the reliefs' with its stucco decoration is undoubtedly the most impressive *(Tue–Sun 8.30am–7pm, in winter till 4pm | admission 6 euros).* The grave goods, weapons and cult items found here are on display in the *Museo Nazionale Cerite* in *Castello Ruspoli,* a Renaissance palace on Piazza S. Maria in Cerveteri *(Tue–Sun 8.30am–7.30pm | free admission).* Directions: Cerveteri, motorway A12 or SS1 Via Aurelia; by train: local train to Ladispoli (direction of Grosseto, approx. one every hour) from Stazione Termini, change to a blue Cotral bus for Cerveteri, then a one-hour walk to the necropolises, in summer a shuttle bus (www.comune.cerveteri.rm.it).

TIVOLI (147 F3) *(𝄽 O)*

Villa Adriana, to be found just before you get to Tivoli, almost 20 miles east of Rome, is surrounded by oaks, pines and cypresses. Fascinated by the impressions he had gained on his travels through the whole Roman Empire, Emperor Hadrian (AD 76–138) built a palace where he could show the highlights of Roman civilisation to his visitors: the Lyceum and Stoa Poikile, the gate of the agora in Athens, large and small baths, the valley of temples in Thessaly and the Nile canal between Alexandria and Canopus. The emperor spent his hours of leisure in the bizarre Teatro Marittimo, a circular temple on an island between his hall of philosophers and a Greek and Latin library. Perhaps he was mourning his beautiful young friend Antinous, who died young and whose statues adorn every corner of the residence *(daily 8.30am until one hour before dusk | admission 6.50 euros).* In the town of Tivoli lies *Villa d'Este* with its amazing water features, which are fed by the *fontana dell'organo idraulico,* a spectacular 'water organ'. Cardinal Ippolito (1509–72) had this terrace-like Renaissance park with its 500 springs and fountains built at the foot of his sumptuous villa *(Tue–Sun 8.30am until one hour before dusk | Piazza Villa d'Este | admission 8 euros).* Directions: take Via Tiburtina, Settecamini to the place called Villa Adriana. By bus: blue Cotral bus from Metro B: Ponte Mammolo to Villa Adriana, 15 min on foot to Hadrian's villa, then a short walk to the C.A.T. bus (shuttle) to

RELAX & ENJOY

If you would like to treat yourself after the rigours of sightseeing, here is an address that will do you good: in the ● *Centro Benessere* in the De Russie luxury hotel you can be pampered while hobnobbing with Rome's high society: sauna, gym, warm Jacuzzi with saltwater for approx. 35 euros, shiatsu massage and facials for around 75 euros. Book in advance! *Centro Benessere La Russie |* Via del Babuino 9 | tel. 0 63 32 88 88 20 | Metro A: Flaminio
More indulgence for body and soul is on offer at the ● *Acanto Day Spa,* where guests enjoy Asian tea, Thai massages and ethereal scents. From 55 euros. *Piazza Rondanini 30 | tel. 06 68 30 06 64 | www.acantospa.it | bus 70, 81, 87, 116, 492*

SIGHTSEEING

The town of Tivoli with the fountains of Villa d'Este makes a great day trip

Tivoli Centro. 5 min to Villa d'Este. Return: Cotral bus to Metro B: Ponte Mammolo (www.comune.tivoli.rm.it).

OSTIA ANTICA & OSTIA
(146 B5–6) (*m O*)
Ostia Antica, a city of ruins less than 20 miles from the Eternal City, was Rome's harbour and naval base at the mouth of the Tiber in the 4th century BC, but the harbour has now silted up. You can stroll beneath pine trees along streets of ancient shops, past the forum with its temples and baths, dwellings, warehouses and the theatre. On the square behind the theatre you can even see an example of ancient sponsoring: nymphs, sea monsters and ships giving advertising space to the commercial enterprises that financed the theatre – all of which already existed in Augustus' time *(Tue–Sun 8.30am until one hour before dusk | admission 4 euros).*

Three miles further on you are in *Ostia* with its beach and disco scene. The water quality has improved in recent years, the beach and pinewoods are cleaner, and there are pools for those who don't like to swim in the sea. *La Vecchia Pineta* is a popular fish restaurant with a terrace overlooking the sea, and also has the usual beach huts *(Lungomare/Piazzale dell'Aquilone 4 | tel. 06 56 47 02 55 | local train: Piramide-Lido di Roma: Castelfusano).*

For night owls who like the idea of going straight from the dance floor for a swim in the illuminated sea, the municipality of Ostia now organises *Il Mare di Notte* (the sea at night). At weekends Ostia and the nearby seaside resorts are of course packed. *Directions: by car take highway 201 or the Via del Mare, or* ● INSIDER TIP *catch a local train for only 1 euro* from Magliana (Metro B) to Ostia Lido to Ostia Antica. *Or from Stazione Ferrovie Roma – Lido di Ostia, Piazzale Ostiense (Piramide).*

FOOD & DRINK

For modern Romans art is not about Baroque style, marble busts and ancient ruins, but about everyday enjoyment of life. Who cares about political crises, strikes and road traffic made in hell as long as mamma cooks the spaghetti *al dente*? Eating, either at home or in a restaurant, is a matter of passion for Italians. The descendants of the famous gourmet and champion banqueter Lucius Lucullus, who came from Rome of course, don't know what a pasta-free day is. Marcus Gaius Apicius, the world's earliest author of cookery books, writing in the 1st century AD, listed 100 different sauces for spaghetti. An Italian pasta shop often has a wider choice than a toyshop. The varieties range from *agnolotti,* pasta stuffed with meat, to half-moon-shaped creations known as *strozzapreti* (priest-stranglers).

Yes, the Italians truly enjoy their food. Breakfast is a modest affair, but it's normal to have two cooked meals a day: lunch and dinner. Until recently the habit of eating several courses was religiously adhered to. In the historic centre tourists have succeeded in changing this custom, and you will be able to get away with ordering just an ample *primo* with a salad. Most Romans now go without their *dolce,* the dessert, and make do with a black *caffè,* what's known as espresso in English. The midday meal is taken between 1pm and 3pm, and in the evenings, restaurants open at around 7.30pm. At this time you can easily get a table, but if you want to eat later, it's advisable to book.

In a ristorante, a trattoria or mamma's kitchen – the people of Rome really know how to enjoy their food

But table reservations will not help much in Rome in January or August, as many restaurants are closed in those months. When it comes to drinking, Italians are traditionally-minded. To accompany a meal they usually order a light house wine *(vino sfuso/vino di casa),* which will be good and cheap – and, it goes without saying, dry. A DOC or DOCG sign on the label is a guarantee of the origin by region or location. White wines made nearby in Castelli Romani, e.g. Frascati, are popular, as is a glass of fresh-tasting Orvieto, Vernaccia di S. Gimignano and dry Verdicchio.

There is no real equivalent to the pub in Italy. The restaurant proprietor will look askance if you order beer but no food. In a pizzeria too they will expect you to order at least a snack. If you like to drink wine, an alternative to going to a restaurant is a *vinoteca,* a wine bar.

Italians make a little ritual about paying for a meal. The waiter brings the bill *(il conto)* – 15 per cent service is usually included – and brings back exact change down to the last cent. If you were satisfied, you leave up to five per cent on the plate. Unfortunately standards of service and courtesy have fallen noticeably in re-

In what was once the studio of the sculptor and architect Antonio Canova you

Goethe, Gogol and Schopenhauer sat here: Antico Caffè Greco

cent years, especially in the tourist zones. Always ask for an official invoice *(ricevuta fiscale),* as tax inspectors sometimes make checks.

CAFÉS & ICE-CREAM PARLOURS

ANTICO CAFFÈ GRECO (137 E1) (*M E7*)
Where Goethe sat and philosophised, Arthur Schopenhauer was shown the door and Nikolai Gogol wrote his Dead Souls, you can still take a seat, order coffee and, when you look at the bill, feel inspired by the muse just like them. *Mon–Fri 9am–7.30pm, Sat–Sun 10.30am–7pm | Via Condotti 86 | Metro A: Spagna*

can enjoy your cappuccino or aperitif between fine works in plaster and marble. But of course they are copies. Even a trip to the WC holds artistic surprises in store. This is a popular stop-off in the upmarket quarter near the Spanish Steps. *Mon–Sat 8am–1pm, after that a restaurant | Via del Babuino 150 | Metro A: Spagna*

INSIDER TIP CAFFETERIA CHIOSTRO DEL BRAMANTE (136 B–C3) (*M D8*)
On a terrace above the elegant Renaissance courtyard built by Bramante you can enjoy coffee or brunch *(Sun from 11am),* have an aperitif from 5pm, browse in the bookshop and view an exhibition. From the *Sala delle Sibille* on the first floor you can also look at a

highlight of the neighbouring church of Santa Maria della Pace: frescoes of the sibyls painted by Raphael. *Tue–Sun 10am–7.30pm | Via della Pace | www. chiostrodelbramante.it | bus 40, 62, 642*

EMPORIO ALLA PACE ●
(136 B3) *(ⳉ D8)*

Literary cafés like Emporio are all the rage with young Romans, who like to snuggle into a soft armchair in the morning with their netbook or tablet, leaf through the fashionable magazines, have a snack or salad at midday and then sit around until late in the evening with a mojito or a glass of rosé. *Daily 7–2am | Via della Pace 28 | www.lemporioallapace. com | bus 40, 46, 62, 64, 81, 87, 116*

GELATERIA GIOLITTI ●
(137 D2–3) *(ⳉ E8)*

Rome's most famous ice-cream salon has been in business since 1900. Traditionalists order the *bacio* chocolate ice cream or the truffle ice. Fruit sorbets, INSIDER TIP champagne flavour and ginger

are also chart-toppers here. It's the haunt of Silvio Berlusconi and half the members of the Italian parliament. *Daily 7–2am | Via Uffici del Vicario 40 | bus 62, 63*

SAID-ANTICA FABBRICA DEL
CIOCCOLATO ● (141 E6) *(ⳉ K8)*

In this old chocolate factory dating from 1923 in San Lorenzo you can do three things: try and buy the creations of the chocolatiers (ricotta-filled chocolates are delicious) – or eat a proper meal. The chefs give all their dishes a finish of chocolate. Or you can sit in the café on a trendy bar stool that's actually a milk churn and sip at hot chocolate so creamy that the spoon stands up on its own. *Mon–Sat | Via Tiburtina 135, corner of Via Marrucini | tel. 0 64 46 92 04 | www. said.it | tram/bus 3, 19*

SAN CRISPINO (137 F2) *(ⳉ F7–8)*

The *limone* ice cream really tastes of lemon here and *amaretto* has all the flavour of almond liqueur. No artificial aromas are added here. It's expensive but irre-

---

★ **Checchino dal 1887**
The international elite dines here in the slaughterhouse quarter → p. 76

★ **Fortunato al Pantheon**
The continuation of politics by culinary means → p. 76

★ **Santa Lucia**
Treats under the trees just behind Piazza Navona → p. 77

★ **La Veranda**
New Roman cuisine in a Baroque courtyard → p. 77

★ **Da Paris**
Traditional Roman food in Trastevere → p. 78

★ **Pierluigi**
Eat on Piazza Ricci with a sparkling prosecco for aperitif → p. 78

★ **Da Franco ar Vicoletto**
A good old trattoria in San Lorenzo → p. 80

★ **Urbana 47**
Slow food but smart food in a trattoria serving regional dishes in Monti → p. 82

MARCO POLO HIGHLIGHTS

sistible. *Wed–Mon 12 noon–0.30am | Via della Panetteria 42 | bus 117*

SANT'EUSTACHIO (137 D3–4) (⌘ D–E8)

The aroma emanating from Rome's oldest coffee roasting establishment wafts over Piazza Sant'Eustachio, where other cafés that roast their own beans have set up shop. The *caffè* comes already sweetened unless you order it *senza zucchero*. *Daily 8.30–1am | Piazza Sant'Eustachio 82 | www.santeustachioilcaffe.it | bus 75, 116*

TRE SCALINI ☆ (136 C3) (⌘ E8)

A cup of *caffè* and to go with it the delicious chocolate truffle *tartufo* ice cream on Piazza Navona. This indulgence is easy on the palate, tough on the wallet. *Thu–Tue 9am–10pm | Piazza Navona 28 | bus 70, 81*

RESTAURANTS: EXPENSIVE

CHECCHINO DAL 1887 ★ (143 D5) (⌘ D12)

This upscale trattoria, which serves hearty Roman food, attracts a high-ranking international clientele. Its specialities are dishes using innards. The wine list is excellent. *Tue–Sat | Via Monte Testaccio 30 | tel. 06 57 43 81 6 | www.checchino-dal-1887.com | bus 95*

FORTUNATO AL PANTHEON ★ (137 D3) (⌘ E8)

Over an elegant meal of fish such as *linguine al pescatore* you can watch Italian politicians indulging themselves. As the seat of government in Palazzo Chigi and the parliament in Palazzo Montecitorio

GOURMET RESTAURANTS

Agata e Romeo (144 C1) (⌘ H8–9)

Creative cuisine, high-class surroundings, specialised in seafood. Try ravioli stuffed with pear and gorgonzola, lentil soup with shrimps or fresh tuna. From 100 euros. Near S. Maria Maggiore. *Mon–Fri | Via Alberto 45 | tel. 06 44 66 11 5 | www.agataeromeo.it | Metro A: Vittorio, bus 71*

Hostaria dell'Orso (136 C2) (⌘ D8)

Medieval columns, frescoes on the walls: Rome's oldest guest house, where Rabelais, Goethe and Onassis once slept, is a top address once again now that three-star chef Gualtiero Marchesi is in charge. Menu from 95 euros. *Only evenings, closed Sun and Aug | Via dei Soldati 25c | tel. 06 68 30 11 92 | www.hdo.it | bus 30, 70, 81, 116*

Il Pagliaccio (136 A4) (⌘ C8)

Head chef Anthony has cooked his way to stardom with Asian-Italian fusion menus. How about scampi and calamari with roasted peanuts in coconut sauce, quenched with green tea? Menu from 135 euros. *Daily, Sun–Tue evenings only | Via dei Banchi Vecchi 130 | tel. 06 68 80 95 95 | bus 62, 64*

La Pergola (138 A1) (⌘ A3)

How did a Bavarian get to be pasta king of Rome? Heinz Beck, voted Rome's best chef for the first time in 1997, has three Michelin stars. His signature dish is langoustine ravioli. The nine-course menu on the ☆ roof terrace with views of Rome and celebrities is a snip at 198 euros. *Tue–Sat | Via Cadlolo 101 | tel. 06 68 80 95 95 | www.romecavalieri.it | bus 907, 913*

Fashionable eatery with a shady garden: Restaurant Santa Lucia just off Piazza Navona

are just round the corner, dining at Fortunato's is a continuation of politics by culinary means. *Mon–Sat | Via del Pantheon 55 | tel. 0 66 79 27 88 | bus 116*

AL MORO (137 E3) (*M F8*)

An upmarket traditional restaurant, excellent for celebrity-spotting, by the Fontana di Trevi. *Spaghetti agli scampi,* lamb and goat kid are the specialities. *Mon–Sat | Vicolo delle Bollette 13 | tel. 0 66 78 34 95 | bus 116, 117*

PRIMO (145 E3) (*M M10*)

If you like having film stars, models and designers sporting a creative look at neighbouring tables, Via del Pigneto's trendy restaurant is the place to be, even though Marco Galotta's down-to-earth Roman cooking – e. g. *gnocchetti* with tomatoes and calamari – is not as creative as his customers. *Tue–Sun | Via del Pigneto 46 | tel. 0 67 01 38 27 | www.primoalpigneto.it | tram 5, 14, 19*

SANTA LUCIA ★ (136 C3) (*M D8*)

No wonder divas as varied as Sophia Loren and Madonna shared a taste for dining here under the trees. Come here to spoil yourself with all kinds of fish or *sciallatielli* (hand-made pasta from Apulia). Behind Piazza Navona. *Daily, in winter only Wed–Mon | Largo Febo 6 | tel. 06 68 80 24 27 | bus 70, 492*

LA VERANDA ★ (138 C5) (*M B7*)

In the Baroque courtyard of the Hotel Columbus near the Vatican you can enjoy modern Roman food, e.g. *orecchiette* with scampi and chicory salad or rabbit chasseur. *Tue–Sun | Via della Conciliazione 33 | tel. 066 87 29 73 | bus 40, 62*

RESTAURANTS: MODERATE

INSIDER TIP ANTICA HOSTARIA L'ARCHEOLOGIA (147 D5) (*M K–L16*)

If you are looking for a nice garden restaurant after a dusty walk on Via Appia Antica, this is it! Wisteria and roses bloom, little fountains gurgle and the pasta dishes, e.g. with fish and mussels, are just superb. *Wed–Mon | Via Appia Antica 139 | tel. 0 67 88 04 94 | bus 118*

COSTANZA (136C4–5) (*D9*)

Within the walls of the ancient Theatre of Pompeius, this hostaria serves game paté, pasta with truffles and Tuscan steaks. If you feel a shiver run down your spine as you eat, perhaps that's because Caesar was murdered by Brutus and his fellow conspirators in 44 BC at Pompey's Column a stone's throw away. *Mon–Sat | Piazza del Paradiso 65 (behind Sant'Andrea del Valle) | tel. 06 86 17 17 | bus 30, 40, 62, 63, 64, 70, 116, 495*

Pasta with langoustine sauce
– Pierluigi's version is delicious

GINAS PICNIC (137 E1) (*E7*)

Gina's is actually a high-class snack bar serving sandwiches of salmon and beef or swordfish carpaccio. But the real sensation here is **INSIDER TIP** Gina's picnic basket to take away to the nearby park of Villa Borghese: luxury rolls, red wine, cheese, fruit, coffee, corkscrew and tablecloth (approx. 40–65 euros). *Via San Sebastiano 7a/Piazza di Spagna | tel. 06 67 80 25 1 | www.ginaroma.com | Metro A: Spagna*

INSIDER TIP OSTERIA DELL'ANTIQUARIATO (136 B3) (*D8*)

You sit close to the Tiber on the pretty piazzetta near Via dei Coronari, enjoy home-made pasta such as *tagliatelle ai carciofi* (pasta with artichokes) and delicious fish dishes. Prices are very reasonable at lunchtime. *Daily | Piazzetta di S. Simeone 26 | tel. 06 68 79 69 4 | bus 40, 46, 62, 64*

DA PARIS ★ (143 D3) (*D10*)

Roman cuisine on one of the traditional squares in Trastevere: *gnocchi* with fish ragout, lamb *(abbacchio alla scottadita)* and pasta with courgette flowers and scampi. *Tue–Sat and Sun midday | Piazza S. Callisto 8 | tel. 06 58 15 3 78 | express bus H, tram 8*

PIERLUIGI ★ (136 B4) (*C–D 8–9*)

The fish, spaghetti in langoustine sauce, carpaccio and chocolate cake are famous locally. Try the dry house Prosecco, *Bernabei, for a bit of sparkle with your meal. Tue–Sun | Piazza dei Ricci | tel. 06 68 68 71 70 66 86 13 02, bus 64, 116*

POMMIDORO (141 F6) (*K8*)

The *letterati* Alberto Moravia and Pier Paolo Pasolini philosophised here over their *spaghetti carbonara* or *all'amatriciana*. The landlord never cashed Pasolini's last cheque, which he wrote the evening before he died. The artists and *glitterati* of San Lorenzo still come here, because Anna and Aldo's Roman-style food is so good. *Mon–Sat | Piazza dei Sanniti 44 | tel. 06 44 52 6 92 | tram/bus 3, 19*

QUATTRO MORI (138 B6) (*U B8*)

When Benedict XVI was still called Cardinal Ratzinger, he liked to go to this trattoria five minutes from the Vatican, where good Sardinian fish dishes are on offer: gilthead sea bream, tuna, swordfish. There are only two menus: *mare,* i.e. fish, and *montagna,* meat, at 35 euros each. *Tue–Sun | Via Santa Maria alle Fornaci 8a | tel. 0 66 39 01 95 | bus 34, 46, 64*

DA UGO (137 D2) (*U E7*)

Although their restaurant is situated between Piazza Navona and the parliament, Ugo and his wife Maria have not let all the prominent neighbours affect their style. For over 30 years they have been serving up good, solid Roman dishes like *bucatini alla matriciana.* Don't come here if you're in a hurry however. *Mon–Sat | Via dei Prefetti 19 | tel. 0 66 87 37 52 | bus 116*

VINCENZO ALLA LUNGARETTA (143 D2) (*U E10*)

A cosy eatery where cannelloni, lasagne and pizza come from the wood-fired oven. Try the imaginative antipasti, stuffed aubergines, pepperoni and artichokes. *Daily | Via della Lungaretta 170/173 | tel. 0 65 80 03 45 | tram 8, bus 780, H*

RESTAURANTS: BUDGET

DA AUGUSTO ● (143 D2) (*U D10*)

One of Trastevere's good old trattorias. When you take a seat on the piazza, the owner Augusto lays out a paper tablecloth and immediately takes your order. If you can't understand his thick accent, simply order the dish of the day from the blackboard, e.g. *coniglio* (rabbit) or *pollo* (chicken). *Mon–Fri and Sat midday | Piazza de' Renzi 15 | tel. 0 65 80 37 98 | tram 8*

INSIDER TIP IL BOCCONCINO ☺ (144 B2) (*U G10*)

Right behind the Colosseum, Giancarlo – who is actually a pharmacist – and his wife Nelly have opened a slow-food trattoria that has been a real hit in the locality. Try their traditional Roman-style starters such as *polpette di melanzane e pinoli,* aubergine dumplings with pine kernels, *crostini di alici,* toasted bread with anchovies, or *spezzatino di vitella,* veal stew with beans. *Thu–Tue | Via Ostilia 23 | tel. 06 77 07 91 75 | tram 3, bus 60, 75, 81, 85, 117*

WHEN IN ROME ...

... do as the Romans do. If you order an ,espresso' in Milan, they are willing to understand, but if that's what you ask for in your favourite bar in Rome, the *barista* behind the counter will raise his eyebrows and check the order: ,Ma Lei vuole un caffè?' So if you want to pass for a local, just say ,un caffè' (the ,è' is stressed but pronounced like the ,e' in ,get', not like ,ay' in ,away'). And if you prefer to drink filtered coffee, ask for ,un caffè americano'.

Eating ice cream in Italy also has established rituals: first the *gelataio* asks whether you want a *cono* or *a coppa,* a cone or a cup. Then you decide the size of the portion according to the price, 2, 3 or 4 euros, (in *bella Italia* not according to the number of scoops) and only then do you choose the *gusti,* the flavours.

LOCAL SPECIALITIES

▶ **abbacchio alla scottadito** – roast lamb with rosemary potatoes
▶ **baccalà** – dried cod, often with peas
▶ **bollito misto** – mixed boiled meats, usually served with a green sauce
▶ **bucatini all'amatriciana** – tube-like pasta pieces with tomato sauce, bacon and pecorino
▶ **carciofi alla giudea/romana** – artichokes fried in oil
▶ **carpaccio di manzo** – thin raw slices of fillet of beef with rocket leaves and Parmesan
▶ **carpaccio di pesce** – thin marinated slices of swordfish or tuna (photo right)
▶ **ciammotta** – deep-fried vegetables
▶ **coniglio alla cacciatora** – rabbit braised in the oven with rosemary
▶ **fave e pecorino** – beans with pecorino
▶ **finanziera** – stew of chicken, sweetbread and mushrooms
▶ **garofolato** – braised beef
▶ **gnocchi salvia e burro** – small potato dumplings with sage and butter
▶ **insalata di puntarelle** – bitter salad leaves with garlic and anchovies
▶ **orecchiette** – ear-shaped pasta, often served with broccoli and scampi
▶ **ortiche** – young nettles as a creamy pasta sauce
▶ **pagliata** – calf's intestines with penne pasta
▶ **panzanella** – white bread with tomatoes, oil and chopped basil as a salad
▶ **panzarottini** – filled pasta baked with cheese and egg
▶ **pasta e fagioli** – penne or other fresh pasta with bean soup
▶ **pesce spada** – swordfish with lemon and oil, usually grilled
▶ **pollo al diavolo** – spicy chicken
▶ **porchetta** – slices of suckling pig on a roll, usually served cold at a stall (photo left)
▶ **saltimbocca** – slice of veal with sage and Parma ham
▶ **scamorza con prosciutto** – smoked cheese with ham
▶ **trippa alla romana** – tripe, usually served with vegetables

DA FRANCO AR VICOLETTO ★
(141 E6) (*ɯ K8*)
For 30 years Franco's regulars in the university and workers' quarter of San Lorenzo have been coming here – originally as students, now accompanied by their children. A three-course menu costs 28.50 euros, INSIDER TIP two courses can be had for 19 euros. *Tue–Sun | Via dei Falisci 3 | tel. 0 64 95 76 75 | bus 71*

GINO E PIETRO (136 B4) (🛱 D8)

A restaurant with a family atmosphere: mamma Adriana often cooks, papà Pietro chooses the best vegetables (the *antipasti di verdure* is a delicious, generous portion), and son Emanuele waits on the diners. Lots of regular guests are proof of good quality. *Fri–Wed | Via del Governo Vecchio 106 | tel. 0 66 86 15 76 | bus 62, 64*

DA GIOVANNI (136 A6) (🛱 C9)

You have to get here early, as this simple little osteria, one of the last of its kind, is very popular with the artisans and other residents of the area. The pasta is of course home-made, and all the wines are sold by the glass or carafe. *Mon–Sat | Via della Lungara 41a | tel. 0 66 86 15 14 | bus 23, 280*

HOSTARIA ROMANESCA (136 C5) (🛱 D9)

Come for the view alone! You are sitting on the sunny side of life here on buzzing, colourful Campo de' Fiori. No sophisticated cooking, just plain Roman dishes like *spaghetti carbonara* and *pollo ai peperoni*. A reservation is necessary in the evenings! *Daily | Campo de' Fiori 40 | tel. 0 66 86 20 24 | bus 116*

SERGIO ALLE GROTTE (136 C5) (🛱 D9)

This wonderfully old-fashioned trattoria is hidden away in an alley off Via Giubbonari behind Campo de' Fiori. Try Sergio's classics such as *spaghetti amatriciana* or *puttanesca*. There's fresh fish on Tuesdays, Fridays and Saturdays. *Mon–Sat | Vicolo delle Grotte 27 | tel. 06 86 42 93 | tram 8, bus 30, 40, 62, 63, 64, 70, 81*

Typical Roman food, served on Campo de' Fiori: Hostaria Romanesca

TRAMTRAM (141 F6) *(Ⓜ L8)*
The name derives from the tram that passes on its way to Porta Maggiore. The cooking is Roman with Sicilian and Pugliese influences e.g. *orechiette alla Norma*, ear-shaped pasta with vegetables, *rigatoni alla pajatina* with calf's intestines, and *gnocchi con baccalà*, i.e. with cod. *Tue–Sun | Via dei Reti 44 | tel. 06 49 04 16 | tram 3, 19, bus 492*

URBANA 47 ★ ⏱ (140 B6) *(Ⓜ G8)*
The ambience in this osteria at the heart of Rome's trendy nightlife quarter of Monti is characterised by retro chic, the diners mainly come from the fashion business, and the food is authentic: home-made pasta and regional dishes made exclusively with local organic products e.g. with *farro* (spelt) and *puntarelle*

(bitter leaves). *Daily | Via Urbana 47 | tel. 06 47 88 40 06 | www.urbana47.it | Metro B: Cavour, bus 117*

VINOTECHE (WINE BARS)

BAR PASQUINO (136 C4) *(Ⓜ D8)*
Get here early, as the Battle of the Buffet starts at 1pm – a stand-up buffet, or seated if you prefer. *Piazza Pasquino 83 | bus 62, 64*

BUCCONE (139 E4) *(Ⓜ E6)*
Where horses were stabled once, exquisite wines are stored today. Enjoy them with light dishes such as pasta and baked aubergines, and an array of high-quality olive oils and balsamic vinegars. *Mon–Thu only midday, Fri–Sat evenings too| Via di Ripetta 9 | tel. 0 63 61 21 54 | Metro A: Flaminio, bus 117, 119*

INSIDER TIP **OBIKÀ** (137 D2) *(Ⓜ E7)*
Cheese with tomatoes, salmon or Parma ham in Rome's first mozzarella bar, where the superb buffalo-milk cheese comes from its region of origin, Campania, and other tasty small dishes accompany the fine wines. *Daily | Via dei Prefetti 26a | tel. 0 66 83 26 30 | bus 81, 117, 119*

AL PARLAMENTO (137 D2) *(Ⓜ E7)*
A stone's throw from their chamber, members of parliament find solace here after political flops and heated debates. *Mon–Sat | Via dei Prefetti 15 | bus 116*

INSIDER TIP **VINOROMA** (139 E4) *(Ⓜ D7)*
With her guided Italian wine tastings, the young sommelière Hande Leimer has created an iconic Roman experience, guiding you through seven Italian wines in her pretty flat on the Tiber. *Daily 5pm by prior arrangement | 50 euros/*

LOW BUDGET

▶ Drink your espresso, cappuccino or orange juice at the counter. Served at a table, especially around the tourist haunts, it can be three times as expensive.

▶ You can get a quick refreshment or cup of coffee for very little money at the souvenir stand run by nuns in the dome of *San Pietro* **(138 B5)** *(Ⓜ A7)*.

▶ Order tavola calda e.g. at Volpetti **(139 E5)** *(Ⓜ D–E7)* (Mon–Sat | Via della Scrofa 31) to get a decent pasta dish for about 8 euros.

▶ Pilgrims queue up in the *Caffè San Pietro* **(138 C5)** *(Ⓜ C7)* for a piatto, a simple dish, for about 8 euros *(daily | Via della Conciliazione 40)*.

Love mozzarella? Then the place to go is Obikà mozzarella bar

person | Lungotevere dei Mellini 10 | tel. 06 32 54 05 12, mobile 32 84 87 44 97 | www.vinoroma.com | bus 30, 70, 81, 492

PIZZERIAS & TAVOLE CALDE (SNACK BUFFETS)

DA BAFFETTO (136 B3) (*D8*)

An established institution close to Piazza Navona. Hungry customers queue here every evening. *Mon–Sat, evening only | Via del Governo Vecchio 114 | tel. 0 66 83 40 24 | bus 62, 64*

IL BOSCAIOLO (140 A4) (*F7*)

Pizzeria north of the Fontana di Trevi with a wide selection of toppings and thin, crispy dough. The salads are good, too. *Tue–Sun evening only | Via degli Artisti 37 | tel. 0 64 88 40 23 | Metro A: Barberini*

ER BUCCHETTO (140 B6) (*G–H8*)

Three plain wooden tables and no choice at all: what Franco makes is genuine *por-*

chetta, a Roman pork dish seasoned with salt, pepper and fennel. The juicy roast revolves on a spit at 270° C (°F 518) and is eaten with white bread. From 5 euros per portion. *Via del Viminale 2 F | Metro A: Termini, B: Cavour, bus 64*

INSIDER TIP GUSTO (139 E4) (*E7*)

Some think Rome's coolest pizzeria is chic, while others compare it with a station concourse, but no one doubts the quality of the pizza. On the 2nd floor there is also a restaurant, and round the corner a wine bar under the same management. *Daily | Piazza Augusto Impera tore 9 | tel. 0 63 22 62 73 | www.gusto.it | bus 81, 117, 119*

DAL PAINO (136 B3) (*D8*)

A newcomer that gets good marks among the pizzerias of the district, but here too you can expect to queue up. *Thu–Tue | Via di Parione 34/35 | tel. 06 68 13 51 40*

SHOPPING

CITY **WHERE TO START?**

A good starting point for shopping is the bus stop on **Largo Chigi/Piazza San Silvestro**, **(135 E2) (▥ E7)** at the end of the pedestrian zone. From here you are within easy reach of the exclusive district of alta moda between Via Frattina, Via Condotti and Via Borgognona continuing to Piazza di Spagna, but you can also stroll along the much cheaper Via del Corso and take a look inside the elegant Galleria Alberto Sordi shopping arcade. Metro A: Spagna, bus 52, 53, 61, 62, 63, 71, 80, 85, 95, 116, 119, 175, 492

A for *alta moda*, 'high fashion': from Zegna to Armani, from Valentino to Byblos, in Rome even the children know the designers' alphabet backwards.

Italian fashion is a major export item. You will find it in London, Berlin or New York too, but in Rome you have come to the source. Shopping around classy Piazza di Spagna, home to Gucci, Prada, Versace, Dolce e Gabbana, is like leafing through Vogue magazine, and exclusive streets like Via Condotti and Via Borgognona, where the tailors to the rich reside in historic palazzi, can seduce you into a stylish shopping spree. Nearby in Via del Babuino there is a mix of expensive men's fashion with antique shops, lamps and furniture design. But don't overlook side streets such as Via Mario de' Fiori or Bocca

Photo: High-class shopping at Nuyorica

Rome is home to the Caesars of fashion: *alta moda* in old palazzi and trendy boutiques, but also lots of design and craft products

di Leone, where you can find small, high-class purveyors of moda uomo, men's fashion, that are not always as expensive as you might think. Like Milan, Rome too now has an elegant arcaded shopping mall, at the corner of Via del Corso and Via del Tritone: ● INSIDER TIP *Galleria Alberto Sordi* with cafés and upmarket stores. To get a fashionable outfit at a reasonable price, Via del Corso is a good hunting ground. Affordable boutiques for bags and accessories have recently started to pop up around the Pantheon.

Many shops are open daily from 10am to 8pm, but some close at midday between 1pm and 4 or 5pm, especially in the summer heat. In winter everything stays closed on Monday morning – except the food shops.

ANTIQUES

APOLLONI (139 F4) (*∅ E6*)
Renowned gallery for classical art, from tables made of Carrara marble to a Rococo writing desk. *Via del Babuino 132–134 | Metro A: Spagna, bus 117*

ORGANIC FOOD STORES & MARKETS

DI CASTRO (139 F4) *(🗺 E6)*
Beautiful prints and paintings *(Via del Babuino 71)* as well as antiques *(Piazza di Spagna 5)*. Metro A: Spagna, bus 117

LA CHIOCCIOLA (136 B3) *(🗺 D8)*
La chiocciola means 'the snail', but this shop is specialised in gilded putti, marble statuettes and ancient urns. Via dei Coronari 186 | bus 30, 70, 81, 87, 116

MAURIZIO GROSSI ★ (139 F4) *(🗺 E6)*
Venus de Milo, busts of Caesars or an obelisk for your living room? Copies of

Volpetti: an institution for gourmets

artworks from antiquity, decorative and conveniently sized. *Via Margutta 109 | www.mauriziogrossi.com | Metro A: Spagna, bus 117*

ORGANIC FOOD STORES & MARKETS

ALBERO DEL PANE ⏱ (137 D5) *(🗺 E9)*
Rome's oldest health-food shop has all kinds of organic foodstuffs, juices vegeta-

bles and environmentally sound washing powders and detergents, as well as a big range of natural cosmetics. *Via S. Maria del Pianto 20 | www.romabiologica.com | tram 8, bus 30, 63, 70, 780*

BIOMARKT ⏱ (136 B4) *(🗺 C8)*
Twice a month organic farmers from the surrounding area sell their eco-products: fruit, vegetables, honey, cheese, wine and olive oil. There are stands with wooden toys and clothes made from organically grown cotton. *2nd and 4th Sun, 9am–5pm | Vicolo della Moretta | bus 116*

DIMENSIONE NATURA ⏱
(137 D5) *(🗺 C8)*
This fashion shop near the Fontana delle Tartarughe on Piazza Mattei aims to combine ecological textiles made from cashmere, alpaca, linen and silk with chic Roman style. *Via dei Falegnami 66 | tram 8, bus 30, 40, 63, 64, 70*

BOOKSHOPS

FELTRINELLI
A publisher with three modern bookshops and an excellent range of international literature. *Via del Babuino 39/40* (139 F4) *(🗺 E6) | Metro A: Spagna; Via E. Orlando 84* (140 B5) *(🗺 G7) | Metro A: Repubblica; Largo di Torre Argentina 5a* (137 D4) *(🗺 E9) | also Sun 10am–1.30pm, 4–7.30pm | bus 62, 64*

ANGLO-AMERICAN BOOKSTORE
(137 E1) *(🗺 E7)*
The huge stock encompasses art and architecture, history and literature. The department for science and technology is down the street at no. 27. *Via delle Vite 102 near the Spanish Steps | Metro A: Spagna, bus 116, 117, 119*

MEL (140 B6) *(🛈 G8)*
A big but well-ordered assortment of books ranging from literature to art and computing. *Via Nazionale 254 | Metro B: Piazza Repubblica, bus 64*

FINE FOODS

ANTICA SALUMERIA (137 D3) *(🛈 E8)*
Roman delicacies such as sheep's and goat's cheese, Parma ham, olives, top wines and delicious pizza. *Piazza della Rotonda 3/Pantheon | bus 116*

INSIDER TIP **ENOTECA ANTICA**
(137 E1) *(🛈 E7)*
A distinguished shop dating from 1905 selling vintage champagne, red and white wine and rare liqueurs. You can try the wines and eat a snack *(evenings only | tel. 0 66 79 08 96) | closed Mon | Via della Croce 76a | Metro A: Spagna*

FOCACCI (137 E1) *(🛈 E7)*
Focacci stocks treats like dried ceps, truffles, olive oil, wine and grappa. *Via della Croce 45 | Metro A: Spagna*

VOLPETTI (143 E4–4) *(🛈 E12)*
Rome's chefs come here to buy excellent ingredients: a full range of Italian cheeses and hams, olive oil of the finest quality. At the counter you can eat a refined snack at midday. *Via Marmorata 47 | Metro B: Piramide, bus 3, 8, 23, 30, 75, 280*

GIFTS

ALDO FEFE ★ (137 D2) *(🛈 E7)*
This shop for classy stationery and bookbinding has been in business since 1932. Aldo, the owner, produces your personal books, albums or frames within two days. *Via della Stelletta 20b | bus 62, 64, 81, 87, 116*

CAMPO MARZIO DESIGN (137 D2) *(🛈 E7)*
High-class fountain pens and colourful notebooks made from top-quality leather. *Via di Campo Marzio 41 | www.campomarziodesign.it | bus 116, 117*

MARCO POLO HIGHLIGHTS

INSIDER TIP **TECH IT EASY**
(137 E2) (*E8*)

Everything the digital heart desires: clocks that show all time zones, unusual bathroom scales, electronic knick-knacks | *Via del Gambero 1 and Galleria Alberto Sordi | www.tech-it-easy.it | bus 52, 53, 61, 71, 80, 85, 117*

TEMPI MODERNI (136 B4) (*D8*)

Retro look: bracelets and necklaces in Sixties style, outlandish ties and hip bags. *Via del Governo Vecchio 108 | bus 62, 64*

LAMPS & DESIGN

ARTEMIDE (139 F4) (*E6*)

From Tolomeo table lamps to Alfiere hanging lumieres in silver and the Arcadia bedside lamp – at Artemide's they are switched on to the latest trends. *Via Margutta 107 | www.artemide.com | Metro A: Spagna*

NORA P ★ (144 A1) (*G8*)

A stylish bathtub filled with flowering orchids or colourful deckchairs to brighten up your front room. Nora Pastore's design store brings new ideas even to trendy Monti. *Via Panisperna 220 | www. nora-p.com | Metro B: Cavour, bus 117*

MARKETS & FLEA MARKETS

MERCATINO FLAMINIO (139 E2) (*D5*)

Clothes, clothes, and more clothes, including vintage fashion at a popular flea market with 240 stands. *Piazza della Marina 32 | Sun 10am–7pm | admission 1.60 euros | tram 2, 19*

PORTA PORTESE ★
(143 D3–4) (*D11*)

You can find almost anything here – possibly including your stolen wallet, though of course it will be empty. Hats, shoes, binoculars, watches, out-of-the-ordinary clothing. And watch out for pickpockets!

Anything second-hand, clothes and lots of kitsch: Porta Portese flea market

Sun 7am–2pm | between Viale Trastevere and Porta Portese | bus 780, tram 8

ARMANI (137 E1) (*ロ E7*)

His career plan was originally to become a surgeon, but then Giorgio Armani decided to operate in the world of fashion. His creations, whether a business outfit, the youthful Emporio line, perfumes or lifestyle products, are synonymous with Italian good taste. *Via Condotti 76 | www. giorgioarmani.com | Metro A: Spagna*

ARSENALE (136 B4) (*ロ D8*)

Cutting-edge but not all that expensive. Designer fashion by Patrizia Pieroni with an art gallery. *Via del Pellegrino 172 | bus 64, 116*

BORSALINO

Gangsters, gigolos and gentlemen have worn it: for 150 years the broad-brimmed borsalino has been the definitive hat. *Piazza del Popolo 20* (139 E3) (*ロ E6*) | *bus 117, 119 and Piazza Fontana di Trevi 83* (137 E–F3) (*ロ F8*) | *www.borsalino. com | bus 62, 63, 85, 116, 117, 119*

CALEFFI (137 D–E3) (*ロ E8*)

Shirts and suits made to measure for politicians and ordinary mortals. *Via della Colonna Antonina 53 | bus 62, 63, 81, 85, 116, 117*

INSIDER TIP CUCINELLI (137 E1) (*ロ E7*)

Brunello Cucinelli from Umbria not only makes the very best cashmere pullovers, but also has a reputation as a businessman with a social conscience. His factory is a former country estate in the pretty village of Solomeo, which he has restored from top to bottom. This style has rubbed off on his new flagship boutique in Via Borgognona. But you pay *prezzi alle stelle*, which is Italian for exorbitant!

Via Borgognona 33 | bus 52, 53, 61, 62, 83, 71, 80, 116, 119

EDO CITY ★ (144 A1) (*ロ G9*)

In Monti, fashion designer Alessandra Giannetti turns out suits for women, linen raincoats and casual trousers in subtle pastel colours in her very own Japanese-Italian style. *Via Leonina 78 | www.edoc ity.it | Metro B: Cavour, bus 117*

FENDI ★

The five Fendi sisters rule over an empire of furs, fashion and cosmetics with a showroom in a glass palazzo on the Corso. *Via Borgognona 36–40* (137 E1) (*ロ E7*) and *Largo Goldoni* (137 D1) (*ロ E7*) | *www.fendi.com | bus 117*

FURLA (137 E1) (*ロ E7*)

In 1955 Aldo and Margherita sold their first leather bags for self-confident women. The upmarket bag producers from Bologna have opened a new store on Rome's most exclusive shopping street. *Via Condotti 55 | www.furla.com | bus 61, 62, 63, 117*

LE GALLINELLE (144 B1) (*ロ G8*)

Imaginative ways of making something old into something new: in Monti, Wilma Silvestri recycles fabrics and transforms them into fantastic fashion. *Via del Boschetto 76 | Metro B: Cavour*

GENTE (139 F4) (*ロ E6*)

Chic and eccentric clothes for people who are at the forefront of fashion. It costs nothing to look. *Via del Babuino 82 | bus 117*

GUCCI ★ (137 E1) (*ロ E7*)

Leather bags, fashion and accessories by this well-known Italian luxury brand. *Via Condotti 8 | www.gucci.com | Metro A: Spagna*

FASHION FOR YOUNG PEOPLE

MASSIMO DUTTI (137 E2–3) (𝄞 E8)
The very best here is for men, the women's collection can't quite match it. *Galleria Alberto Sordi (Galleria Colonna), corner of Corso and Tritone | www.massimodutti.com | bus 62, 63, 116, 117, 119*

MAX MARA (137 E1) (𝄞 E7)
Lots of smart things to wear by an Italian designer who took over his parents' tailor's shop 60 years ago and made it into a fashion empire. *Via Condotti 19/20 and 46 Via Frattina 28 | Metro A: Spagna*

NUYORICA (136 C4) (𝄞 D9)
Stars like Cameron Diaz do their shopping here. The prices will make you gasp, but it's fun to look inside, and that's free. *Piazza Pollarola 36/37 | bus 40, 63, 63, 116*

SCALA QUATTORDICI ★ (136 B6) (𝄞 C–D10)
Very stylish and far from mainstream. If you have some imaginative ideas of your own for a suit, skirt or dress, Maria will make it for you in only ten days. *Via della Scala 14 | tram 8*

TALARICO (136 B3) (𝄞 D8)
This traditional Neapolitan tailor makes the top-end ties and cravats that Berlusconi and Bill Clinton wear. *Via dei Coronari 52 | bus 40, 62, 64*

VALENTINO (137 E1) (𝄞 E7)
One of the last grand aristocrats of the fashion business, who helped to invent the dolce vita and at the age of almost 80 still rules his empire. *Via Bocca del Leone 15 (men), Via Condotti 12–13 (women) | Metro A: Spagna*

LOW BUDGET

▶ For affordable shopping head for *Via Giubbonari* (136 C5) (𝄞 D9), *Via del Corso* (137 D1/E2) (𝄞 E6–8), *Via del Tritone* (137 E–F2) (𝄞 F7), *Via Nazionale* (140 A6/B5–6) (𝄞 F–G 8–9) or *Via Cola di Rienzo* (138 C–D4) (𝄞 B–D6).

▶ Designer fashion, sometimes at half price: *Discount dell'Alta Moda* (139 E4) (𝄞 E6) (*Via del Gesù e Maria 14–16 | Metro A: Spagna, bus 117*).

▶ At the clothing market in *Via Sannio* (144 C3–4) (𝄞 J11) (*Mon–Sat morning*) you will find the women of Rome and lots of truant schoolkids hunting for bargains. *Piazzale Appio | Metro A: S. Giovanni*

FASHION FOR YOUNG PEOPLE

CASA DELLE CINTURE (136 C5) (𝄞 D9)
Wide or thin, leather, glossy, crocodile or zebra look: if you want to belt up, this is the place. *Via dei Giubbonari 60/61 | bus 30, 40, 62, 63, 81, 492, tram 8*

DIESEL (137 D1) (𝄞 E7)
The number-one store for ragazzi, with laser lights and a dance-club atmosphere. *Via del Corso 185 | Metro A: Spagna*

METTEMI GIÙ (137 F1) (𝄞 F7)
Jackets, trousers, jeans: colourful and laid-back, a casual look for children. *Via dei due Macelli 59e | Metro A: Spagna, bus 117*

LA SELLA (139 E3–4) (𝄞 D8)
Fashionable leather bags, purses and wallets, belts, all at affordable prices. *Via della Cuccagna (Piazza Navona) | bus 40, 46, 62, 64, 116*

Bulgari sells jewellery, watches and accessories with a VIP cachet

JEWELLERY

BULGARI (137 E1) *(🕮 E7)*
The window display is restrained, and the real treasure store is inside. No price tags: if you have to ask, forget it! *Via Condotti 10 | Metro A: Spagna*

HEDI MARTINELLI (139 F4) *(🕮 E7)*
If you are looking for unusual jewellery made from gold, silver and copper, or corals and semi-precious stone, then this is the right address. *Via Mario de' Fiori 59b | Metro A: Spagna*

MELIS (136 C2) *(🕮 C8)*
Goldsmith Massima works with 21-carat gold for his regular customers, and produces modern items from 2000-year-old coins. *Via dell'Orso 57 | bus 116*

INSIDER TIP R-01-IOS
(145 D2) *(🕮 M10)*
The name is not a secret code, but identifies the flagship store of Iosselliani, Rome's most far-out pair of jewellery designers, Roberta and Paolo in Pigneto. Their second shop, T-02-IOS, is in Tokyo's Shimbuya district. *Via del Pigneto 39a | www.iosselliani.com | tram 5, 19*

SHOES

BORINI (136 C5) *(🕮 D9)*
Top-quality made-to-measure shoes, almost too good to wear: this is a high-end shoemaker for Rome's elegant circles. *Via dei Pettinari 86 | bus 23, 116, tram 8*

TOD'S (137 D1) *(🕮 E7)*
Diego della Valle is celebrated as the inventor of gommini, smart moccasins eminently suitable for driving. Having succeeded in making Tod's a coveted brand for girls on the make and ambitious young managers, della Valle recently made headlines as a patron of the arts by donating 25 million euros for restoring the crumbling Colosseum. *Via Fontanella Borghese 56/57 (Largo Goldoni) | bus 117*

ENTERTAINMENT

CITY **WHERE TO START?**
If you want to see the happening scene, go to **Pigneto**. Around Via Pigneto **(145 E–F3) (∅ M10)** there are more film clubs, book bars and creatively styled dance clubs than anywhere else. The downside is that Pigneto has fairly poor transport connections at night. As long as Metro C line is still under construction, you'll need a taxi back to the city centre.

***Dolci notti* (sweet nights) in Rome's open-air museum between the Vatican, Spanish Steps and Pantheon?**
On balmy evenings from April to October nightlife in Rome still takes place in the narrow streets of the Centro Storico. Although there are lots of bars, cafés, wine bars and clubs, most young Romans prefer to stroll around the streets until the early hours, passing enchantingly illuminated ancient buildings, licking an ice cream, refreshing themselves at bubbling fountains and greeting their friends on all sides – almost always in large groups, as Romans don't like to be alone. As well as the city centre and Trastevere, **INSIDER TIP** Monte Testaccio too has kept the charm of old-time Rome but is nevertheless a fashionable scene – just like the workers' and students' quarter San Lorenzo, and the Monti and Garbatella districts. And for some time now the nightlife has spread to the lower-profile district of Pigneto on two main roads out of the city,

Photo: Hot music at Alibi

Trastevere, Testaccio and the clubbing scene – but for young people in Rome, the real nightlife happens on the street

Via Prenestina and Via Casilina. For up-to-date information about cinema, theatre and events refer to the Thursday supplement *Trova Roma* in the daily newspaper *La Repubblica* and in the weekly guide *Roma c'è*. You can also get information from *www.comune.roma.it* and *www.abcroma.com*.

BARS, CAFÉS & WINE BARS

Most night bars have an admission charge in the shape of a membership pass *(tessera)* for approx. 15 euros, or otherwise 20–30 euros. Just occasionally the first drink is free.

BAR DEL FICO (136 B3) *(⌕ D8)*
A really cool bar – but don't dress too smartly. A shabby Brit-pop look fits better. *Daily | Piazza del Fico 26 | bus 64, 116*

BEVITORIA NAVONA (136 C3) *(⌕ D8)*
This wine bar is so tiny that you might easily overlook it, but inside it can be so cosy that nobody wants to leave. In the cellar

you see the remains of the ancient stadium on which Piazza Navona was built. *Mon–Sat | Piazza Navona 72 | bus 70, 81, 116*

A trendy hang-out during the day or evening: Caffè della Pace

INSIDER TIP ▶ LA CABALA
(136 C2) (*₥ D8*)

John Wayne once drank his companions under the table here with whisky, and Aristotle Onassis looked deep into Maria Callas' eyes. Following a thorough refurbishment, this legendary nightclub is once again a rendezvous for celebrities. *Wed–Sat | Via dei Soldati 25c | tel. 06 68 30 11 92 | bus 70, 116, 492*

CAFFÈ LATINO ★ (143 D5) (*₥ D–E12*)

A buzzing location in the vaults of Monte Testaccio. *Tue–Sun | Via di Monte Testaccio 96 | tel. 0 65 72 85 56 | www.caffelatino diroma.com | bus 95, 170, 781*

CAFFÈ DELLA PACE ★ ●
(136 B3) (*₥ D8*)

Crowds of the beautiful people inside and outside. Good for a *caffè* during the day, and in the evening for drinks and cocktails. *Daily | Via della Pace 3–7 | bus 62, 64*

CAVOUR 313 (140 B6) (*₥ G9*)

A genuine Italian wine bar with stylish people, tasty snacks and fresh salads. *Daily, closed Sun in summer | Via Cavour 313 | Metro B: Via Cavour*

CUL DE SAC (136 C4) (*₥ D8*)

Popular with a young crowd. Apart from pasta there are all sorts of other things to eat. *Daily | Piazza Pasquino 73 | bus 62, 64*

FLUID (136 B4) (*₥ B4*)

Currently the place to be among Rome's cocktail and wine bars. Near Piazza Navona. Good DJs, electric house music and an ample buffet at the blue hour from 6pm. *Daily | Via del Governo Vecchio 46/47 | www.fluideventi.com | bus 40, 46, 62, 64, 116*

FONCLEA (136 A1) (*₥ C7*)

A classic address among the live music bars in the Prati quarter. Jazz, rock, Dixie blues and funk every night. *Daily, closed July–Aug | Via Crescenzio 82 | www.fon clea.it | bus 34, 49, 87, 492*

INSIDER TIP ▶ FRENI E FRIZIONI
(136 B6) (*₥ D10*)

Until recently this was a little car repair shop in Trastevere where *freni e frizioni* (brakes and clutches) were fixed. Now it's a popular bar for well-lubricated conversation. *Daily | Via del Politeama 4–6 | bus 23, 280, H, tram 8*

JONATHAN'S ANGELS (136 B3) (*₥ D8*)

In this cult bar near Piazza Navona owner Jonathan has painted INSIDER TIP ▶ lavish frescoes on the walls – even in the toilets! *Tue–Sun | Via della Fossa 16 | bus 62, 64*

PICASSO CAFÉ ⭐

(143 D5) (*ΩD–E 12–13*)

Much frequented by artists and would-be artists, used for literary readings and spontaneous music performances. *Mon–Sat | Via di Monte Testaccio 63 | tel. 0 65 74 29 75 | bus 95, 170, 781*

IL PICCOLO (136 C4) (*ΩD8*)

Well-attended wine bar with a wide choice. Try the *prosecco rustico*. *Daily | Via del Governo Vecchio 74 | bus 62, 64*

RIVE GAUCHE 2 (141 F6) (*ΩL8*)

A cross between a café, pub and disco, at the heart of the San Lorenzo student quarter. Happy hour till 9pm. *Daily | Via dei Sabelli 43 | tel. 0 64 45 67 22 | tram 3, 19, bus 71, 30*

TARTARUGHINO (136 C3) (*ΩD8*)

Upmarket piano bar. Customers drink their cocktails wearing a white suit or their little black evening dress in classical surroundings. Live music from 10pm.

Mon–Sat | reservations tel. 06 68 64 31 | Via della Scrofa 1 | bus 116

DANCE CLUBS

ALIBI (143 D5) (*ΩD13*)

Rome's oldest-established gay disco with an enormous dance floor and roof terrace. You can have a film made of yourself dancing and download it at home. *Wed–Sun | Via di Monte Testaccio 44 | tel. 0 65 74 34 48 | bus 95, 170, 781*

BLACKOUT (O) (*ΩM10*)

Just like the name says: black is what the teenagers here wear, and the music too is black. And there's also punk, rock, grunge and house. *Tue–Sat | Via Casilina 713 | tel. 0 62 41 50 47 | bus 105*

FANFULLA 101 ⭐ (O) (*ΩM10*)

Pasolini, the Sixties film director with an unconventional lifestyle, would have loved this retro joint and underground arts centre in Pigneto, his favourite quarter. Live indie, jazz, rock, J-pop and art-house films. *Daily | Via Fanfulla da Lodi | www.myspace.com/fanfulla101 | bus 81, 105, 810*

⭐ **Caffè Latino**
1968 atmosphere in Testaccio
→ p. 94

⭐ **Caffè della Pace**
Styled all over: see Rome's chic people → p. 94

⭐ **Picasso Café**
An arty location with poetry readings and music → p. 95

⭐ **Fanfulla 101**
This place throbs – an underground arts centre in Pigneto → p. 95

⭐ **Qube**
Mega-disco in spectacular surroundings in Tiburtino → p. 96

⭐ **Alexanderplatz**
Where the jazz stars play – very close to the Vatican → p. 97

⭐ **Caruso Caffè**
Fiesta, salsa, Cuban son – sometimes live → p. 97

⭐ **Auditorium Parco della Musica**
Hyper-modern concert hall for international big names → p. 98

MARCO POLO HIGHLIGHTS

DANCE CLUBS

GILDA (137 E1) (*ⓜ E–F7*)
Well-established fashionable club where politicians from across the spectrum, B-list celebrities, well-heeled young business people and suburban *ragazzi* rub shoulders. Closed in summer, when everyone moves to *Gilda* in Fregene (*www.gilda onthebeach.it*). *Thu–Sun | Via Mario die Fiori 97 | www.gildabar.it | Metro A: Spagna*

happy hour from 7pm. *Opening times depend on programme, Thu–Tue | corner of Via Pietro Micca 7a and Via Giolitti 7a | tel. 06 87 44 00 79 | www.miccaclub.it | Metro A: Vittorio Emanuele*

QUBE ★ (0) (*ⓜ 0*)
A large-scale club in an old factory, east of the city centre in Tiburtino, with a

Men without a tie don't get in: the glamour-and-glitter disco Gilda

GOA (0) (*ⓜ E15*)
Disco in Ostiense (near Università Roma 3) decked out in Bollywood style. A mix of oriental divan and club-lounge-restaurant. The music is funk and house. *Tue–Sun | Via Libetta 13 | tel. 0 65 74 82 77 | www. goaclub.eu | Metro B: Garbatella, bus 770*

INSIDER TIP ▶ MICCA CLUB (144 C1) (*ⓜ J9*)
Surrounded by the columns of what was once a wine cellar behind Stazione Termini, quality DJs do their stuff and young mojo, pop and rock stars call by. Often

transgender programme: *RadioRock* on Thursdays, the gay show *Muccassassina* on Fridays, *Babylon for all* on Saturdays. *Wed–Sat | Via di Portonaccio 212 | tel. 06 43 85 44 50 | www.qubedisco.com | bus 409, 440, tram 5, 14, 19, get out at Prenestina/Via Portonaccio*

RADIO LONDRA (143 D5) (*ⓜ E13*)
This themed bar named after an Allied radio station from the Second World War is absolutely in. The ambience is an improvised air-raid shelter with sandbags lying all around. It goes without saying that

the bar staff wear helmets. *Wed–Mon | admission 15 euros | Via di Monte Testaccio 67 | tel. 0 65 75 00 44 | bus 95, 170, 781*

ROOM 26 (O) (*⌘ O*)

An ambitious project by a group of young people who are mad about music and art on Piazza Marconi. The programme ranges from clubbing to a restaurant and exhibitions of modern art and photos. *Thu–Sun | Piazza Marconi 31 (EUR quarter) | www.room26.it | bus 30, 714, 791*

JAZZ, FOLK & LATIN

ALEXANDERPLATZ ★
(138 B4) (*⌘ A–B6*)

Italy's oldest jazz club, where almost all the great names have played, is still swinging in Prati. *Mon–Sat | admission 15 euros | Via Ostia 9 | tel. 06 39 74 21 71 | www.alexanderplatz.it | Metro A: S. Pietro, bus 492, 495, tram 19*

CARUSO CAFFÈ ★
(143 D5) (*⌘ D–E13*)

Fiesta, live bands, the hot tip for salsa, merengue, tango or Cuban son. Most Thursdays the band *Chirimia* plays. *Tue–Sun 10.30pm–3am | Via del Monte Testaccio 36 | tel. 0 65 74 50 19 | www.caruso cafe.com | bus 95, 170, 781*

CASA DEL JAZZ (143 F5) (*⌘ F12*)

A mafia boss once lived here, and his confiscated villa with large park is now a venue for jazz, jam sessions, festivals. *Viale di Porta Ardeatina 55 | tel. 06 70 47 31 | www.casajazz.it | Metro B: Piramide, bus 714*

CINEMAS & OPEN-AIR CINEMAS

AZZURRO SCIPIONI (139 D3) (*⌘ C6*)
Well-loved art-house cinema with film weeks devoted to avant-garde mov-

ies and international retrospectives from Robert Altman to Akira Kurosawa and Luchino Visconti. Some screenings with subtitles. *Via degli Scipioni 84 | tel. 06 39 73 71 61 | www.azzurroscipioni.com | Metro A: Lepanto*

INTRASTEVERE (136 B6) (*⌘ D10*)

Film club in an alley near Piazza Trilussa in Trastevere, often screening films in the original English version. *Vicolo Moroni 3a | tel. 0 65 88 42 30 | bus 3, tram 8*

NUOVO SACHER (143 D3) (*⌘ D11*)

The production of cult director Nanni Moretti is called Sacher, and his own cinema is Nuovo Sacher – a declaration of his love for the Viennese cake of that name. **INSIDER TIP** In summer cinema under the stars. Sometimes discussions with the directors. *Largo Ascianghi 1 | tel. 0 65 81 81 16 | www.sacherfilm.eu | tram 3, 8*

THEATRE, OPERA, MUSICALS & CONCERTS

At last Rome can hold its head high vis-à-vis other great cities for classical music, theatre and opera. After eight years of excavation and construction – delayed not only by archaeological finds but also by the usual scandals – the city has a concert hall worth its salt, the *Auditorium Parco della Musica.*

You can still hear good orchestras and choirs performing in the appropriate surroundings of a church, especially in the winter months. In Baroque churches such as ● *Sant' Ignazio, Santa Maria del Popolo* and *Santa Maria in Aracoeli* form the stage for organ concerts and oratorios, with a wonderful atmosphere and for free. Sometimes the walls of the Pantheon reverberate to the sound of Gregorian chants. For opera and concert listings, see *www.musicaroma.it*

AUDITORIUM PARCO
DELLA MUSICA ⭐ (147 D4) (∅ D2)

A superb complex for concerts. During construction of this three-part building designed by Renzo Piano the founda-

tions of a Roman villa were discovered. They have been skilfully incorporated into the architecture. The Auditorium has three halls seating 2800, 1200 and 700 people which are connected by foyers and lead to an open-air amphitheatre. The people of Rome are delighted with their new concert halls, whether they come to listen to a classical star like pianist Maurizio Pollini or improvisations by Keith Jarrett. The complex includes a cafeteria and a large shop for music and

JAZZ IN A TRAM

● Rumble through Rome at night in a tram dating from 1947 while a jazz band plays or a few young opera singers belt out arias. The finishing touch is that the trams stops to let you dine with a view of the lit-up Colosseum. The food with fresh regional products and good wines is from the 🙂 *Palatium* slow-food restaurant. The three-hour *TramJazz* trip starts from Porta Maggiore every Friday and Saturday at 9pm. *Price 65 euros per person, reservations essential: www. tramjazz.com, www. romeguide.it, www. listicket.it or tel. 06 89 29 82.*

Auditorium Parco della Musica: ultra-modern architecture for music by Renzo Piano

books, as well as a park with playground. *Park daily 11am–8pm | exhibition about musical themes 1 euro | www.auditorium roma.com | tickets tel. 06 89 29 82, from abroad tel. +39 0 53 70 01 06 | box office Thu– Tue 11am–6pm | Viale Pietro de Coubertin 15 (near Stadio Flaminio) | www.listicket.it | bus 53, 217, M, tram 2, 19*

TEATRO ARGENTINA (137 D4) (𝄞 E8)

The neo-Classical theatre on Largo Torre Argentina hosts performances by Italy's best ensembles, while young directors show what they can do at the avant-garde branch *Teatro India* (143 D5) (𝄞 E9), a former factory on the banks of the Tiber (near Stazione Trastevere). *Box office daily 10am–2pm, 3–7pm | Largo di Torre Argentina 5 | tel. 0 66 87 54 45 | www.teatrodiroma.net | bus 62, 64; Teatro India | Lungotevere dei Papareschi | bus 170, H, 780 (Piazza Radio), tram 8*

TEATRO MARCELLO

(137 D–E6) (𝄞 E9)

Concerts of chamber music, *concerti del tempietto,* are held after dark in the ancient amphitheatre. *Via del Teatro di Marcello 44 | tickets tel. 0 64 81 48 00 | www. estateromana.comune.roma.it, www. operaroma.it | bus 30, 63, 170*

TEATRO DELL'OPERA

(140 B5) (𝄞 G8)

It may not be La Scala in Milan, but in 1990 the opera in the *Terme di Caracalla* (144 B4–5) (𝄞 G12), which was otherwise known for its mediocrity, was made world-famous by the three tenors José Carreras, Plácido Domingo and Luciano Pavarotti. Following a ten-year closure the impressive Baths of Caracalla have reopened, and in summer some performances are held there. *Box office Tue–Sat 9am–8pm | Piazza Beniamino Gigli 1 | tel. 06 48 07 84 00 | www.helloticket.it | Metro A: Repubblica*

WHERE TO STAY

Rome's hotel categories are a lottery, and their stars are not always a guarantee of quality.

Be prepared for little surprises: dark rooms, lukewarm coffee for breakfast, the whine of mopeds at night, showers without shower curtains and sometimes thick-skinned staff who deflect complaints with a regal manner.

If this happens to you, stay calm: in Rome it's different things that matter, for example the *grandezza* of the lobby with all its marble, plaster ceilings and perhaps a pretty courtyard. In some hotels a wonderful view from the top floor makes up for the dripping tap. And don't worry too much if the hotel breakfast is modest, to put it mildly, as you are much better advised to do what the locals do:

drink a cappuccino and eat a fresh croissant in a nearby bar.

The pricing system in hotels is often mysterious. The prices displayed on a notice in reception and in the room are to be seen as net prices, to which 19 per cent VAT, breakfast, and in summer often a supplement for air conditioning, are added. As prices of accommodation have rocketed to the extent that they have overtaken those in Paris, many hotels make *offerte speciali* via internet outside the peak season. A double room for less than 100 euros in the Centro Storico, the historic city centre, is a rarity in the high season. It's not surprising that many visitors are now opting for bed & breakfast, which costs between 80 and 180 euros per double room. For young travellers

Many hotels in Rome have a wonderful setting – but beware, as there is no guarantee they are quiet

there are hostels offering a bed from 25 euros per night.

The historic city centre is closed to through traffic from 7am until 7pm and after 10pm, but as there are many residents in this area with their own vehicles, this is no guarantee that things will be quiet. If you have sensitive hearing, when you reserve ask for a quiet room *(una camera tranquilla)* looking out to the rear.

HOTELS: EXPENSIVE

BORGOGNONI (137 E2) *(ω F7)*
Well-appointed hotel in a 17th-century palazzo that has kept its Baroque style. Close to Piazza S. Silvestro. *50 rooms | Via del Bufalo 126 | tel. 06 69 94 15 05 | www.hotelborgognoni.it | bus 63, 492*

CAPO D'AFRICA (144 B2) *(ω H10)*
New four-star hotel in a bright palazzo of the late 19th century, situated in a quiet street behind the Colosseum and

the church of S. Clemente. Pleasant roof terrace for breakfast and sitting in the sun. *65 rooms | Via Capo d'Africa | tel. 06 77 28 01 | www.hotelcapodafrica.com | Metro B: Colosseo, bus 85, 117, 119, tram 3*

RAPHAËL ⭐ (136 C3) (*m D8*)
An atmospheric old palazzo just off Piazza Navona. Some rooms are modern, others furnished with art and antiques. Roof terrace with a panoramic view. *83 rooms | Largo Febo 2 | tel. 06 68 28 31 | www.raphaelhotel.com | bus 70, 81, 492*

HOTELS: MODERATE

CAMPO DE' FIORI (136 C5) (*m D9*)
Here you are really in the thick of the action: in the morning the Campo is Rome's most popular market, in late afternoon the place for an *aperitivo* and in the evening a rendezvous for young Romans. This boutique hotel has small rooms equipped with antiques as well as WiFi, and can also book apartments for up to four persons close by. Great view from the roof terrace. *23 rooms | Via del Biscione 6 | tel. 06 68 80 68 65 | www.hotelcampodefiori.it | bus 40, 46, 62, 64, 116*

CASA VALDESE (139 D3) (*m C–D6*)
Close to St Peter's, boasting a quiet location in the Prati quarter in a late 19th-century villa of the Waldensian church. Cosy atmosphere and **INSIDER TIP** lovely roof terrace. *33 rooms | Via A. Farnese 18 | tel. 06 32 15 3 62 | www.casavaldese roma.it | Metro A: Lepanto*

CISTERNA (143 D2) (*m D10*)
This charming hotel with a pretty courtyard is situated in one of Trastevere's old cobbled alleys. *20 rooms | Via della Cisterna 8 | tel. 06 58 18 52 | www.hotel cisternarome.com | tram 8, bus H*

Wild vine growing outside, full of art inside: the exclusive Hotel Raphaël

HOTEL ART ⭐ (139 F4) (*m E6*)
Rome's coolest design hotel in a historic building lies in the peaceful artists' alley of Via Margutta near the Spanish Steps. The modern rooms are decorated in yellow, blue and orange. Lounge bar and gym. *47 rooms | Via Margutta 56 | tel. 06 32 87 11 | www.hotelart.it*

CONDOTTI (137 E1) (*m E7*)
Stylish hotel that attracts antique dealers and people from the fashion business. *21 rooms | Via Mario de' Fiori 37 | tel. 06 67 94 66 1 | www.hotelcondotti. com | Metro A: Spagna*

FARNESE ★
(139 D3) (*Ⓜ C6*)

Pretty old villa in the Prati district, not far from the Pope's residence. Friendly service, and a good breakfast buffet, by local standards, with a ☀ view. *23 rooms | Via A. Farnese 30 | tel. 0 63 21 25 53 | www. hotelfarnese.com | Metro A: Lepanto*

MODIGLIANI ★
(140 A5) (*Ⓜ F7*)

Excellent location near Via Veneto, quiet, tastefully furnished. See if you can book ☀ INSIDER TIP suite 602 with its rooftop view. Small courtyard garden. *24 rooms | Via della Purificazione 42 | tel. 06 42 81 52 26 | www.hotelmodigliani. com | Metro A: Barberini, bus 52, 637*

NERVA ★
(144 A1) (*Ⓜ F9*)

This charming family-run hotel is ideally placed just behind Trajan's Forum and thus close to the Capitol and Colosseum. *19 rooms | Via Tor dei Conti 3 | tel. 0 66 78 18 35 | www.hotelnerva.com | Metro B: Cavour, bus 64*

HOTEL PRATI (138 C4) (*Ⓜ C7*)

Small rooms but a central location near the Vatican. The service is friendly and manager Luigi Caporuscio knows what visitors to Rome are looking for. *23 rooms | Via di Crescenzio 89 | tel. 0 66 87 53 57 | www.hotelprati.com | Metro A: Ottaviano, tram 19, bus 429*

RAFFAELLO (140 C6) (*Ⓜ G8*)

A small and elegant three-star hotel in the trendy Monti quarter. Quiet rooms with modern bathrooms and a good breakfast buffet, near Stazione Termini. *41 rooms | Via Urbana 3–5 | tel. 0 64 88 43 42 | www.hotelraffaello.it | Metro B: Cavour, bus 117*

RICHMOND (144 A1) (*Ⓜ F9*)

Small, pretty three-star hotel between the Colosseum and Trajan's Forum. From the ☀ terrace you get INSIDER TIP a wonderful view of the Forum Romanum. Babysitters available for the evening. *13 rooms | Largo C. Ricci 36 | tel. 06 69 94 12 56 | www.hotelrich mondroma.com | Metro B: Colosseo, bus 75, 87, 11*

SANT' ANSELMO/VILLA SAN PIO ★
(143 E4) (*Ⓜ E11*)

Two quiet, well-kept Art Nouveau villas on the Aventine Hill with individually furnished rooms and nice gardens. *45 and 80 rooms | Piazza S. Anselmo 3, Via S. Melania 19 | tel. 06 57 00 57 | www.aven tinohotels.com | Metro B: Circo Massimo*

★ **Hotel Art**
Cool design and spacious rooms in an old palazzo → p. 102

★ **Raphaël**
A top address, just off Piazza Navona → p. 102

★ **Farnese**
Stay here to be close to the Vatican → p. 103

★ **Modigliani**
Small and elegant near Via Veneto → p. 103

★ **Nerva**
A romantic location behind Trajan's Forum → p. 103

★ **Sant' Anselmo/Villa San Pio**
Art Nouveau villa on the green Aventine Hill → p. 103

MARCO POLO HIGHLIGHTS

HOTELS: MODERATE

SANTA MARIA (142–143 C–D2) (*🗺 D10*)
A pretty three-star hotel in a 16th-century building at the heart of Trastevere that used to be a monastery. You take breakfast by the orange trees in the courtyard. *18 rooms | Vicolo del Piede 2 | tel. 06 58 94 62 6 | www.htlsantamaria.com | tram 8, bus H*

SMERALDO (136 C5) (*🗺 D9*)
Attractive guesthouse in a central location in the lanes around the church of Sant' Andrea della Valle. Two small 🌿 terraces with a view of the city. *35 rooms | Via dei Chiodaroli 11 | tel. 06 68 75 92 9 | www.smeraldoroma.com | bus 62, 64*

TEATRO DI POMPEO (136 C5) (*🗺 D9*)
A quiet night's sleep above the walls of the ancient theatre where Julius Caesar was murdered 2000 years ago. Centrally situated near Campo de' Fiori. *28 rooms | Largo Pallaro 8 | tel. 06 68 30 01 70 | www. hotelteatrodipompeo.it | bus 40, 60, 64*

TRASTEVERE (143 D3) (*🗺 D10*)
Tiny refurbished hotel five minutes from Santa Maria in Trastevere with a view of the market, which will help you to wake up early. Mini-apartments for up to five people are available too. *9 rooms | Via Luciana Manara 24 | tel. 06 58 14 713 | www.hoteltrastevere.net | bus H, tram 8*

LUXURY HOTELS

Hassler Villa Medici (137 F1) (*🗺 F7*)
The Spanish Steps at your feet, the gardens of the Villa Medici on one side, and the dome of St Peter's almost visible from your pillow. Monarchs and international celebrities have stayed in this long-established hotel. 🌿 Excellent roof-top restaurant with a view. 103 rooms and suites. From 450 euros. *Piazza Trinità dei Monti | tel. 06 69 93 40 | www.hotelhasslerroma.com | Metro A: Spagna*

Lord Byron (139 F1) (*🗺 E4*)
The smallest of Rome's top-class hotels occupies a converted monastery near the park of Villa Borghese, with the exquisite restaurant *Sapori* and only 50 stylishly furnished rooms and suites. From 380 euros. *Via Giuseppe de Notaris 5 | tel. 06 32 20 4 04 | www.lordbyron hotel.com | tram 3, 19*

De Russie (139 E3–4) (*🗺 E6*)
Five-star address at the foot of the Pincio hill near Piazza del Popolo. From the outside it seems an almost modest 19th-century palazzo, but it has a stunning garden created by Giuseppe Valadier on the roof terrace with fountains and statues, a gym and Rome's best spa. 125 rooms and suites. From 620 euros. *Via del Babuino 9 | tel. 06 32 88 81 | www.hotelderussie.it | Metro A: Flaminio, bus 117, 119, 490*

Rome Cavalieri 🌿 (146 C4) (*🗺 A3*)
Luxury hotel belonging to the Waldorf-Astoria group on Monte Mario with the exquisite La Pergola restaurant on the roof, a pool, tennis courts and a fine view over the city. Popular with well-known names from the world of international sport. 387 rooms and suites. From 405 euros. *Via Cadlolo 101 | tel. 06 35 09 1 | www.romecavalieri.it | bus 907, 913*

Lots of greenery and luxury: the historic terrace garden of the Hotel De Russie

VILLA GLORI (0) (*D3*)

Elegant mid-range hotel, four-star standard, with a sensationally low price, especially for internet bookers. The reason is that it is not in the historic centre but in the middle-class Flaminio district, which has good transport connections. Very close to the futuristic MAXXI museum, the Parco della Musica concert hall and the Stadio Olimpico (good if you like football). *52 rooms | Viale del Vignola 26/ Via B. Celentano 11 | tel. 06 32 27 65 8 | www.villagloriroma.com | Metro A: Flaminio, then tram 2, bus 910*

ZARA (140 A5) (*G7*)

A good address just behind Palazzo Barberini and less than ten minutes from the famous Fontana di Trevi. *28 rooms | Via delle Quattro Fontane 37 | tel. 06 48 14 8 47 | www.hotelzara.com | Metro A: Barberini, Repubblica*

HOTELS: BUDGET

ANTICO BORGO (143 D3) (*D10*)

Tiny hotel in a little alley in Trastevere. The rooms are small and not very bright, but the view is superb, and it's fairly quiet for Trastevere. *11 rooms | Via del Buco 7 (near Piazza del Drago) | tel. 06 58 83 37 74 | www.hotelanticoborgo.it | tram 8, bus H*

APOLLO (144 A1) (*G9*)

Small, good-quality, and a great location in trendy Monti, less than five minutes from the Colosseum and Forum Romanum. A good breakfast is served in the pretty ☼ roof garden with a view of the city centre. *24 rooms | Via dei Serpenti 109/Via Panisperna | tel. 06 48 85 88 9 | www.hotelapollorome.com | Metro B: Cavour, bus 40, 60, 64, 117*

HOTELS: BUDGET

AZZURRA (140 A5) (*F7*)
No great luxury, but a first-class location near the Fontana di Trevi. *Via del Boccaccio 25 | tel. 06 47 46 53 31 | www.hotel azzurra.com | Metro A: Barberini, bus 52, 53, 60, 61, 62, 492*

BERGAMO (140 C6) (*H8*)
Centrally located two-star hotel a stone's throw from Termini railway station and the Metro. Standard levels of comfort, WiFi and TV. The nightlife of Monti is within walking distance and the prices, varying according to the season, are low. *23 rooms | Via Gioberti 30 | tel. 06 46 46 49 88 | www.activehotels.com (search: Hotel Bergamo) | Metro A/B: Termini, bus 40, 64, 170, 175, H, M*

LOW BUDGET

▶ Affordable apartments and studios are on offer at *www.friendlyrentals. com/Rome* and *www.only-appartments. com/Rome*. Bargains like a 4-room flat for 6 people at 180 euros near the Vatican Museums, however, are booked out before you can say Hail Mary.

▶ A popular address for young people is *Village Flaminio* **(147 D3)** (*O*) in the north of Rome, a campsite in green surroundings with a pool. *Bungalow sleeping 5 from 132 euros | Via Flaminia Nuova 821 | tel. 06 33 32 60 04, 063 33 14 29 | info@villageflaminio. com | local train towards Prima Porta from Piazzale Flaminio, the stop is Due Ponti | by car: from GRA Gran Raccordo Annulare uscita (exit) 6 in the direction of Flaminio/Roma Centro, as far as Corso Franci*

INSIDER TIP ▶ CASA DELLA PALMA (141 F6) (*K8*)
Only a modest sign on the door reveals this little gem, tucked away in a courtyard in San Lorenzo. The rooms are furnished with new wooden floorboards, marble bathrooms and stylish beds. No reception. *6 rooms | Via dei Sabelli 98 | tel. 06 44 54 42 64 | mobile/cell 033 97 42 27 88 | www.casadellapalma. it | tram 3, 19*

EDERA (144 B–C2) (*H10*)
Elegant little Art Nouveau hotel between the Colosseum and Piazza Vittorio Emanuele. The rooms have been refurbished, and some of them are furnished with antiques. You can reach the Lateran on foot or by tram. Small garden. *28 rooms | Via A. Poliziano 75 | tel. 06 70 45 38 88 | www.leonardihotels.com/Edera | tram 3*

GRIFO (144 A1) (*G9*)
Basic guesthouse with three- and four-bed rooms as well as doubles, offering breakfast on the roof terrace in the romantic Monti quarter. *Via del Boschetto 144 | tel. 06 48 71 39 95 | www.hotelgrifo. com | Metro B: Cavour, bus 64, 117*

IVANHOE (144 B1) (*G9*)
Reasonably priced little hotel at the heart of Monti with all its pubs and down-to-earth atmosphere. The Colosseum and Forum Romanum, Santa Maria Maggiore and the Termini station are within walking distance. Small rooms, roof terrace. *26 rooms | Via Ciancaleone 49/ Via Urbana | tel. 06 48 68 13 | www.hotel ivanhoe.it | Metro B: Cavour, bus 71, 117*

KATTY (138 D5) (*H–J7*)
Spacious and clean rooms in a central location at a good price. What more do you need? *18 rooms | Via Palestro 35 | tel. 06 44 41 12 16 | www.hotelkatty.it | bus 492*

KRISTI (140 C4) (*🗺 H6*)
Pleasant, modest guesthouse for young people, tiny rooms but well-situated near the HQ of the unpopular tax authorities and the popular state president in the Quirinal Palace. *Via Collina 24 | tel. 06 47 44 90 02 | www.romehotelkristi.it | Metro A: Repubblica, bus 16, 60, 61, 62, 63, 84, 90, 492*

LOCANDA CARMEL (142 C3) (*🗺 C10*)
Basic rooms and a wonderful roof garden in Trastevere. *11 rooms | Via Mameli*

py to be cosy in the 1.20 m bed in the single room. There are doubles, also three- and four-bed rooms. *Via Giulio Cesare 47 | tel. 06 30 04 33 31 | www.pensione paradise.com | Metro A: Lepanto, bus 70, 590, 913, tram 19*

BED & BREAKFAST

In recent years more and more bed & breakfasts have opened up in Rome, organised through agencies like the *Bed and Breakfast Association of Rome (tel.*

Its style is almost fashionable again, and the location is fantastic: Hotel Mimosa

11 | tel. 06 58 09 99 21 | www.hotelcarmel. it | bus H, 75, 780, tram 8

MIMOSA (137 D4) (*🗺 E8*)
The furniture is worn but the staff are cheerful. Right by the Pantheon. *11 rooms | Via Santa Chiara 61 | tel. 06 68 80 17 53 | www.hotelmimosa.net | bus 64, 116*

INSIDER TIP ▶ PARADISE (138 C3) (*🗺 B4*)
Owner Luigi is straight-up and easy to deal with. There's no breakfast but a fair discount for young couples who are hap-

06 55 30 22 48 | www.b-b.rm.it); Tomas b&b lets five rooms (80–100 euros) near the Vatican (Viale Giulio Cesare 183 | tel. 06 65 35 85 55 | www.tomas bbrome.com | Metro A: Ottaviano); Anne & Mary offer three well-kept rooms (100–150 euros) close to the Colosseum (Via Cavour 325 | tel. 06 66 99 41 87 | www. anne-mary.com). Natalia Bianchi (mobile/cell 03 39 21 42 00 09 | www.dolce roma.it) has two flats near the Colosseum. The following are also worth a look: www.rometourism.com, carefully selected apartments and rooms; www.*

caffelletto.it, accommodation in high-class houses. For further addresses: *www.*

If you want to stay in Trastevere, book early

bb-roma.it, tel. 0 66 14 83 88, and *www. bedandbreakfastroma.com.*

MONASTERIES

Roman Catholic pilgrims who require cheap accommodation should apply to the local archdiocese in their home country. The accommodation pages of *www. romeguide.it* include a list of religious institutions.

CASA INTERNAZIONALE DELLE DONNE 🙂 (142 C1) *(𝄞 C9)*

For women only: a 16th-century convent in Trastevere is home to the *Forestiera Orsa Maggiore,* the 'Great Bear' women's hostel. Taking up the theme of stars and heavenly bodies, all 13 rooms have female names ranging from Andromeda to Venus. En-suite single rooms *(75 euros).* A night in one of the twelve bright, cheerful dormitories with shared bathrooms costs 26 euros including breakfast, less outside the peak season.

A big plus is the new INSIDER TIP vegetarian *Bio Bio Bar (Tue–Fri 9am–10pm, Sat–Sun until midnight)* in a garden house in the courtyard. Even men are allowed to partake of the vegetarian buffet *(Tue–Sun 12.30–3pm)* or sip an aperitif in the evening, but only until 8.30pm, when the bar is women-only. *Via San Francesco Sales 1a/Via della Lungara | tel. 0 66 89 37 53 | http://www.casainternazionaledelledonne.org/foresteria.htm | bus 23, 280 H*

CASA DI PROCURA DELL'ORDINE TEUTONICO (141 F1) *(𝄞 M2)*

With the nuns of the Teutonic Order in Nomentano, north of the centre with a direct bus connection to Piazza Venezia, you are in good hands. *26 rooms | Via Nomentana 421 | tel. 06 86 21 80 12 | bus 36, 60, 84, 90*

ISTITUTO MARIA SS. BAMBINA (138 B5) *(𝄞 B8)*

This accommodation run by nuns right on St Peter's Square is greatly sought-after by pilgrims, as you can almost look into the Pope's study. So book well ahead, and if you are a night owl, bear in mind that the gate is closed at 11pm in summer. *35 rooms | Via Paolo VI 21 | tel. 06 69 89 35 11 | e-mail: imbspietro@ mariabambina.va | bus 46, 64, 571, 916*

ISTITUTO PADRI TEATINI (136 C4) (𝄞 *D9*)
Specially for youthful pilgrims. Behind S. Andrea della Valle. *Piazza Vidoni 6 | tel. 0 66 86 13 39 | bus 62*

SUORE IMMACOLATE (137 F1) (𝄞 *F7*)
Convent of the Sisters of the Immaculate Conception near the Spanish Steps, with nine rooms. *Via Sistina 113 | tel. 0 64 74 53 24 | Metro A: Spagna*

HOSTELS

In Rome as elsewhere hostels, smarter than the good old youth hostels, are springing up on all sides: with prices starting at 10 euros per person in a dorm they are unbeatable value for young people who don't expect high standards but want to stay somewhere central. Bookings through e.g. *www.hostelworld.com, www.hostelbookers.com*

CIAK HOSTEL (144C2) (𝄞 *J10*)
Cheap hostel near the Lateran. *Viale Manzoni 55 | tel. 06 70 03 14 23 | www.ciakhostel.com | Metro A: Manzoni*

LA CONTRORA (140 B4) (𝄞 *G7*)
A popular overnight stay from 26 euros. *Via Umbria 7 | tel. 0 69 83 73 66 | www.hostelsclub.com | Metro A: Barberini*

PENSIONE OTTAVIANO HOSTEL (138 B4) (𝄞 *B6*)
Rome's oldest hostel has seen generations of backpackers: here they can dump their packs right by the Vatican. *Via Ottaviano 6 | tel. 06 39 73 81 38 | www.pensioneottaviano.com | Metro A: Ottaviano*

BOOKS & FILMS

▶ **Imperium** – Robert Harris' historical thriller about the great Roman orator and lawyer Marcus Tullius Cicero (2006) is hard to put down, and the sequel (*Lustrum*, 2009), is equally good. Harris' excellent knowledge of ancient Rome makes his work more than just good light entertainment

▶ **La dolce vita** – Federico Fellini's cult film (1960) shows its age, of course, but the scene in which Anita Ekberg and Marcello Mastroianni get in the Fontana Trevi just has to be seen

▶ **Estate romana, (Roman Summer)** – about three sensitive losers who live together, with Rome providing the background noise; a film by Matteo Garrone (2000)

▶ **Roman Tales** – Alberto Moravia (1959) conveys an impression of the teeming life of Rome after the Second World War. His best-known novel, *The Woman of Rome* (1949), is about the life of a woman on the streets of Rome under Mussolini who turns to protitution

▶ **Pope Joan** – Donna W. Cross' version (1996) of a popular legend: Joan of Ingelheim dresses as a monk, leaves her German convent for Rome and eventually becomes pope

▶ **The Genius in the Design** – Jakes Morrissey wrote this gripping account (2005) of the rivalry between Bernini and Borromini, the two artists who shaped Baroque Rome

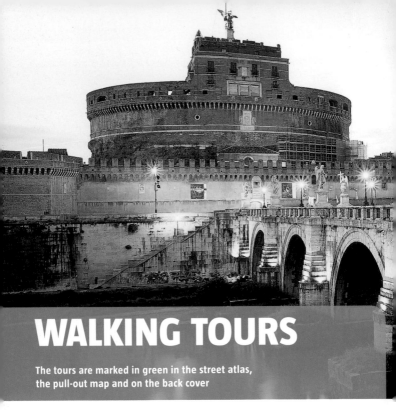

WALKING TOURS

The tours are marked in green in the street atlas,
the pull-out map and on the back cover

1 BAROQUE: FROM VILLA BORGHESE TO ST PETER'S SQUARE

Without them the Rome we know would not exist! The architect and sculptor Gianlorenzo Bernini (1598–1680) and architect Francesco Borromini (1599–1667) couldn't stand each other – but between the two of them they turned the city into a superb Baroque stage. Until his tragic suicide the morose Borromini intrigued against Bernini, a man with a sunny disposition who found that fame, wealth and women fell into his lap. Bernini, who served eight popes over a 60-year career, won the duel. Duration: at least three hours; best time: Sunday morning, when the traffic is lighter.

Start your *Tour de Baroque* at the Galleria Borghese → p. 50 *(don't forget you have to book tickets in advance!),* the best place for getting an impression of Bernini's early works as a sculptor, from the somewhat clumsy-looking David to the radiant nakedness of Apollo and Daphne. Stroll through the gardens of Villa Borghese → p. 54 and across Via Vittorio Veneto, the street of the dolce vita, to Piazza Barberini, where Bernini made his mark twice.

At the corner of Via Veneto and Via Basilio splashes the 'bee fountain', the Fontana delle Api. Three bees were the heraldic symbol of the Barberini family, which brought forth a number of popes. On the piazza Bernini's elegant Fontana del Tritone → p. 48 with its sensuous

Whichever side of the Tiber you choose to do a tour on – the Eternal City is a wonderful place to walk around

Neptune seems to spread a feeling of lightness of being.

When you turn into the steep Via Quattro Fontane, note on the left the three-storey façade of **Palazzo Barberini**, at which Borromini tried his hand first. However it was his arch-rival Bernini whose harmonious synthesis of Doric, Ionic and Corinthian columns won the day. Today this palace is the **Galleria Nazionale d' Arte Antica → p. 50**. At the crossing with four fountains, turn into the long Via Quirinale, where you can see another example of the poisoned but creative rivalry between the two architects. In the little church of **San Carlo → p. 52**, often known by the Romans as **San Carlino**, Borromini, with sparing use of materials, achieved a graceful but austerely composed oval interior that creates an illusion of height.

His colleague Bernini – as usual – was anything but sparing in his means. The two-storey wedding church of **Sant'Andrea al Quirinale → p. 52** less than 200 m further on, also oval but with the longer axis set laterally, has an impressive, monumental entrance and steps. Beyond it is the massive, conspicuous **Fontana dei Dioscuri**, not Baroque but from ancient times, on which colossal statues of the Dioscuri Castor and

designs were drawn up by a certain Gianlorenzo Bernini?

Now cross Via del Corso, walk over **Piazza Colonna → p. 44** with its **Column of Marcus Aurelius**, and you are now in the political arena of modern Italy. Pass

With a splendid backdrop, Neptune rules the waters and the coins thrown into them: Fontana di Trevi

Pollux, taken from the Baths of Constantine, hold on to an obelisk that Emperor Augustus brought back from Egypt as a souvenir.

From ⋰⋰ **Piazza del Quirinale** you can enjoy a wide-ranging panorama before passing the **Palazzo del Quirinale → p. 51** to descend the low steps of Via Dataria. Soon you will hear the splashing of the **Fontana di Trevi → p. 50**. Rome's most sensuous fountain was built by Nicolas Salvi, but did you know that the

Palazzo Chigi, the seat of government, and continue to **Piazza Montecitorio**, which is adorned with obelisks. The curving façade of **Palazzo Montecitorio**, designed by Bernini in 1655, appears every evening on the Italian TV news, as it is the seat of the national parliament, a place of intrigue, back-stabbing, wobbly coalitions and frequent changes of government.

By way of the **Pantheon → p. 44** you come to the small and intimate **Piazza**

S. Eustachio, where the bar of the same name gives you not only what is said to be the best coffee in Rome, but also a view of Borromini's bizarre masterpiece Sant'Ivo della Sapienza. The church with a Baroque façade oscillating between convex and concave curves has the ground plan of a bee. The architect hoped to flatter his immodest patron, Urban VIII, with this reference to the heraldry of the Barberini family.

After crossing Corso Rinascimento you reach Piazza Navona → p. 44, the centrepiece of which is Bernini's Fontana dei Quattro Fiumi. The church of Sant'Agnese is – you guessed it – by his enemy Borromini. Next take Via dei Coronari, once the street of the rosary makers and now in the hands of antique dealers, on your way to the Tiber, where Emperor Hadrian built the bridge in AD 136 to give access to his mausoleum, on top of which the papal fortification Castel Sant' Angelo → p. 56 stands. It was Bernini who made it Rome's most graceful bridge, now named Ponte S. Angelo, by adding serene statues of angels to whom he lent sensuous folds of drapery and a coquettish smile that is more of this world than the next.

The last stop on our walk is the apotheosis, Bernini's boldest work, completed in 1667 in a Christian spirit: Piazza San Pietro → p. 60. This ellipse-shaped square seems to embrace all of Christendom with open arms.

A ROMANTIC ROUTE: TRASTEVERE, GIANICOLO AND THE TIBER

When you have seen so many museums and ancient forums that your head is reeling and your feet are sore, and you yearn to see some nature and get a far view, then look for some relaxation on the 275 ft-high Gianicolo hill, which is dedicated to the Roman Janus.

Start the walk in Trastevere, an old artisans' quarter. Stroll through Via della Lungaretta or one of the other lanes until you come to Piazza Santa Maria in Trastevere, named after the oldest church in Rome that's dedicated to the Virgin Mary → p. 64. The golden mosaic over the narthex sparkles as you approach.

Follow Via della Paglia and then Via Garibaldi as far as the church of San Pietro in Montorio → p. 64. The dainty Tempietto by Bramante in the courtyard of the adjoining Franciscan monastery is a miniature masterpiece of High Renaissance architecture.

Continue on Via Garibaldi (or take the shortcut via the steps of S. Pancrazio) until you hear the rushing of water in the Acqua Paola. In 1612 Pope Paul V commissioned Carlo Maderno to build these bombastic fountains, which were supplied from the restored aqueduct from imperial times. If you can arrange it, get to ⚜ Piazza Garibaldi at noon. Here a cannon salute is fired as in days gone by at exactly 12 o'clock. From the square with the striking equestrian statue of Giuseppe Garibaldi (1807–82), a hero of Italian liberation, the view is stunning. There are cavaliers cast in bronze all over the world, but it's not often you see a INSIDER TIP statue of a female rider. Walk across to the woman who is seated on her horse, a pistol in her hand and her son in her arms. This is Anita Garibaldi Ribeiro, a Brazilian woman who travelled from one country to another at the side of the Italian freedom fighter, bore children and lost them – for the sake of the freedom of South America.

Make one last stop on this walk for a ter-

rific view in the monastery of S. Onofrio. Finally descend via Salita S. Onofrio
to Piazza delle Rovere, where the Tiber
and the traffic await.

3 ANCIENT ROME: VIA APPIA ANTICA

Never on a Sunday? On the
contrary! A Sunday or a holiday is the ideal day to plan a
trip to the 'Queen of Roads',
because that is when the ★ *Via Appia
Antica*, which sees heavy traffic on week-
days, turns into a pedestrian zone and
an (admittedly bumpy) bike trail.

2300 years ago emperors, generals,
merchants, officials and columns of legionaries passed along Rome's most important traffic artery, which the censor
Appicus Claudius Caecus built in 312 BC
to the port of Brindisi. Today cars roar
along this road, which is only 4.30 m
wide. There are no pavements, so beyond Porta S. Sebastiano walkers are
brutally pushed to the wall.

But on Sundays and holidays from 9am
until 7pm the beautiful Via Appia is
closed to cars from the Quo Vadis church
and becomes the oasis of peace that
this archaeological sensation deserves
to be – even if not all Romans observe
the closure – and is suitable for a tour by
bike INSIDER TIP (cycle hire *Sun 9.30am–
5pm | tel. 06 51 35 31 | opposite the Quo
Vadis church).* This ancient military road,

Mass in the Catacombs of Domitilla on Via Appia Antica

lined by tombs from antiquity, three of the five main catacombs, aqueducts and many houses that were illegally built in the 1960, was made into an archaeological park in 1997.

From Porta San Sebastiano you descend gently at the Field of Mars to the little Quo Vadis church, where Via Ardeatina branches off. According to a legend St Peter, fleeing from Nero's executioners, encountered Christ here. When he asked 'Lord, where are you going?' ('Quo vadis?'), he received the answer 'To Rome, to be crucified a second time'. A detour onto Via Ardeatina takes you to the ● Catacombs of Domitilla and Calixtus *(Domitilla: Wed–Mon 9am–12 noon and 2.30–5pm | admission 8 euros | Via Sette Chiese 283/Via Ardeatina; San Callisto: Thu–Tue 9am–12 noon and 2.30–5pm | admission 8 euros | Via Appia Antica 110)*, as well as to a memorial to Nazi crimes: in March 1944 the German army shot 335 innocent Romans at Fosse Ardeatine in revenge for an attack on the SS in Via Rastrella.

Back on Via Appia Antica you pass the Basilica and ● Catacombs of San Sebastiano *(Mon–Sat 9am–12 noon and 2.30–5pm | admission 8 euros | Via Appia Antica 136)*. Note on the left an ancient arena, the Circo di Massenzio, and the Grave of Romulo: not Romulus the founder of the city, but a son of Emperor Maxentius who died young in AD 309. The most impressive building on Via Appia is without doubt the battlemented Tomba di Cecilia Metella, the grave of a rich Roman woman, daughter of a general.

The next part of the route, beneath pines and cypresses, is the most attractive. You pass countless graves – in ancient times burials within the city walls were prohibited – covered with ivy, poppies and daisies. The old Roman paving has

Via Appia Antica

been revealed here. Caesar's carriages had such good suspension that the emperor could travel long distances on the ancient surface in comfort, whereas cyclists today face a shaking and rattling that they will not quickly forget. *Bus 218 (from S. Giovanni in Laterano) or bus 118 (from Metro B: Circo Massimo), both to the Catacombs of Sebastian | Archeobus from Piazza Cinquecento (Termini) to the grave of Cecilia Metella daily 8.30am–4.30pm hourly, fare 10 euros*

TRAVEL WITH KIDS

Is Rome hostile to children? It's like every other big modern city, only a bit more so. The traffic is straight from hell, and there are not many places for running around, as playgrounds are few and far between. *Are the Romans hostile to children?* Not in the least. The Italians have so few children themselves that these rarities are cosseted like pandas in the zoo. In a trattoria the kids are stars, and no-one bothers how much mess they make. *Is Rome a good family destination?* Yes, if you take a relaxed approach. You don't have to tick the Foro Romano off your list when the temperature is 40°C. And when you go sightseeing, an ice cream or a family photo with the hunky legionaries at the Colosseum (for 2–3 euros) will put a smile on the face of moaning kids. ● INSIDER**TIP** Show them how to take a drink of water in true Roman style from a *fontanella*, one of the little springs (cover up the jet of water with your hand and position your mouth over the little hole). Even teenagers love Rome if they can go to the flea market at Porta Portese to rummage for cool sunglasses and belts. And how about a INSIDER**TIP** bike tour on Via Appia Antica *(see page 115)*?

BIOPARCO (140 A3) (*Ø F4*)

The stars in the zoo of Villa Borghese are of course the wolves, Rome's heraldic animals, but there are also 200 other species, from giraffes to lizards. This is a good place for small visitors and big animals. *Daily 9.30am–5pm (summer) 9.30am–4pm (winter), Sat–Sun Apr–Oct until 7pm | admission 12 euros, children above 1m in height 10.50 euros | Viale delle Belle Arti | bus 52, 53, 926, tram 3, 19*

JOIN ASTERIX IN THE FORUM

Follow in the footsteps of Asterix on a walk through ancient Rome, taking in the Colosseum and Forum Romanum or the spooky world of the catacombs, or play detective in a historical thriller about Caesar's rise and assassination. The English-language city guides at *Romaculta* can organise individual tours of Rome for families. *Tel. 33 87 60 74 70 | www.romaculta.it*

STATUE PARLANTI

Go in search of the odd-looking little figures, eroded by weather and pollution, called INSIDER**TIP** ,talking statues', which performed a democratic function

Lots of ice cream, pizza and fun –
Rome has great entertainment for kids,
so long as you keep things relaxed

in papal Rome 300 years ago. At night the Pope's subjects could express dissatisfaction with their rulers anonymously through the mouths of the statues. Today still, Romans hang letters and complaints around the neck of *Pasquino* (137 C4) (*Ø D8*) just beyond Piazza Navona (1164). *Madama Lucrezia* in Palazzetto Venezia (137 E4–5) (*Ø E9*) is the only female talking statue. *Abbot Luigi,* on Piazza Vidoni (136 C4) (*Ø E9*), and *Er Facchino,* the porter on Via Lata (137 E4) (*Ø E8*), are quiet figures compared to *Er Babuino,* the baboon. This talkative ape-man squats in the exclusive Via del Babuino, which is named after him, in front of house no. 150 (136 F4) (*Ø E6*).

TEATRO SAN CARLINO (139 F3) (*Ø E6*)

On the covered Pincio terrace in the park of Villa Borghese, the San Carlino puppet theatre stages modern puppet musicals and classical Italian puppet theatre with popular characters from Commedia dell'Arte such as Pulcinella and Harlequin. *Ticket reservations: tel. 06 69 92 21 17 or www.sancarlino.it | Viale dei Bambini 1/Viale Valadier | Metro A: Flaminio, bus 117, 119*

VILLA BORGHESE
(140 A–B2–3) (*Ø E–G5*)

Rome's second-biggest park is a wonderful place of recreation for children. You can cycle or take a rickshaw *(hire at Porta Pinciana from 5 euros/hr),* row a boat on the *laghetto (3 euros for 20 min),* go jogging, have a walk, picnic or use the WiFi to surf on a park bench. For kids from three to ten there is, in addition to the *San Carlino* puppet theatre, the *Casina di Raphaello,* a house for playing in *(Piazza di Siena),* and a children's cinema. In the *Casina dell'Orologio* garden café *(Viale dei Bambini 1)* you can enjoy a good buffet. *Via Pinciana | bus 52, 53, 116, 490, 495, tram 3, 19*

FESTIVALS & EVENTS

Once all the people of Rome went to the seaside in summer. Now the big summer festival *Estate Romana* makes the city attractive at that time of year, especially in the evenings.

For the latest programme of events go to the tourist information pavilions, see the daily newspapers (the best source is *Trova Roma* on Thursdays in *La Repubblica*, including *The Best in Rome* in English) or the weekly *Roma c'è*. Information on the internet in English: *www.romaturismo. it*, *www.comune.roma.it*, *www.abcroma. com*, *www.romamor.it*

HOLIDAYS

1 Jan, 6 Jan Epiphany, **Easter Sunday and Monday, 25 April** (Liberation from Fascism), **1 May** Labour Day, **2 June** Festival of the Republic, **29 June** St Peter and St Paul, **15 Aug Ferragosto,** Assumption of the Virgin, **1 Nov** All Saints Day, **8 Dec** Feast of the Immaculate Conception, **25 and 26 Dec** Christmas

FESTIVALS & EVENTS

JANUARY
On 6 January the white witch ▶ *Befana* comes with presents for the children of Rome, and Piazza Navona is turned into a playground.

FEBRUARY
Rome too has its historic ▶ *carnevale*, although it's not quite as uninhibited as in Venice.

MARCH/APRIL
Second-but-last Sunday in March: ▶ *Rome Marathon* through the Centro Storico, *www.maratonadiroma.it*.
▶ *Urbi et Orbi*: on Easter Sunday hundreds of thousands of pilgrims flock to St Peter's Square to receive the Pope's blessing; on Easter Monday *(Pasquetta)* they make trips into the countryside.

APRIL
Art fair ▶ *Festa d'Arte* in Via Margutta
21 April: ▶ *Rome's birthday* with concerts and fireworks

MAY
▶ *Festa del Popolo* on 1 May, pop concert on Piazza S. Giovanni
▶ *Antiques fair* in Via dei Coronari (again in September)
▶ *Concorso Ippico Internazionale*, horse-jumping on Piazza di Siena

Hot Roman nights – concerts in churches, jazz on a piazza and opera in the Baths of Caracalla

JUNE

2 June: ▶ *Festa della Repubblica* with a military parade on Via dei Fori Imperiali
13 June: ▶ *Feast of St Anthony of Padua* with Mass in Via Merulana
24 June: ▶ *S. Giovanni*, fair for St John's day at the Lateran
29 June: ▶ *Feast of the city's patrons, St Peter and St Paul*, papal mass in S. Pietro when the faithful kiss the feet of St Peter's statue

JUNE–SEPTEMBER

▶ *Estate Romana*, Roman summer, with jazz, concerts, open-air cinema and fashion shows, *www.estateromana.it*
▶ *Mondofitness,* big open-air sport and swimming festival in the Tor di Quinto quarter, *www.mondofitness-roma.it*

JULY

▶ INSIDER TIP *Festa de Noantri*, popular fair in Trastevere in mid-July with a Madonna procession
▶ *Tevere Expo*, fair of the Italian regions on the bank of the Tiber with music, ballet and folklore, usually from July until early August

AUGUST

15 Aug: ▶ *Ferragosto*, when you and the stray cats have Rome to yourselves, because many Romans are on holiday

SEPTEMBER

▶ *Notte bianca,* museum night with concerts, dance, theatre on the 2nd or 3rd Saturday
▶ *Romaeuropa,* festival of music, theatre and dance from states of the EU

NOVEMBER

▶ *Rome Film Festival,* in the Auditorium Parco della Musica

DECEMBER

8 Dec: ▶ *Feast of the Immaculate Conception* with prayers by the Pope at the Marian column on Piazza di Spagna
▶ *Christmas Market* on Piazza Navona

LINKS, BLOGS, APPS & MORE

LINKS

▶ www.vatican.va/various/cappelle/sistina_vr/index.html This is the best opportunity to see the Sistine Chapel without the crowds and at your leisure, with an accompaniment of beautiful church music.

▶ www.clubsrome.com The English version of a site much used by young Romans: up-to-the-minute tips about the clubbing scene, as well as jazz and concerts.

▶ www.listicket.it Are you looking for a ticket for a concert, a football match or the JazzTram, a high-class evening meal in a restored historic tram? Book here online (English version available).

▶ www.romeby.com As well as accommodation pages you will find useful information about markets, supermarkets and pharmacies that are open 24 hours.

▶ www.romaculta.it Roman art historians who know the Eternal City inside out offer a wide range of tours on interesting historical and arty subjects.

▶ www.blogs.com/topten/top-10-rome-blogs/ Useful selection of favourite Rome blogs about restaurants, literature, art, fashion, ...

BLOGS & FORUMS

▶ www.spottedbylocals.com/rome Five young Roman media professionals have put their recommendations for restaurants, nightlife and events online, paying attention to the less-known quarters of the city. Here are some addresses that don't feature elsewhere, including some places that are hard to find.

Regardless of whether you are still preparing your trip or already in Rome: these addresses will provide you with more information, videos and networks to make your holiday even more enjoyable

▶ www.youtube.com/watch?v=cbrxofJE9gs Omaggio a Roma – director Franco Zeffirelli's ravishing short video about Rome with arias by Andrea Bocelli and appearances by Monica Bellucci.

▶ www.youtube.com/watch?v=qLMMmJzDvR8 Get a insider's view of Zaha Hadid's ultra-modern MAXXI museum. This five-minute video introduces the bold architecture of the new museum of contemporary art.

▶ www.youtube.com/watch?v=Vqw4dAK4usw See how 'Mamma Roma', the wonderful Anna Magnani, lived, cooked and spoke her mind 60 years ago in a typical Roman tenement. A clip from Luchino Visconti 's film Bellissima.

▶ www.youtube.com/watch?v=UxCw9klo-78 What happened when Asterix and Obelix went to Rome? This clip from the film of the classic comic is still entertaining for visitors to Rome. See how the Gauls got on in the Colosseum.

▶ Italian food and drink. You never again need to throw up your hands at the sight of the menu in Italian. Mobilingua tells you in a trice what you'll get if you order crostini di alici or cozze gratinate.

▶ Talking Italian Phrasebook. Free app by CoolGorilla that doesn't need an internet connection to spell out the basics on food, accommodation, transport and romance.

▶ www.facebook.com/pages/Rome/27359671110 Link to the Facebook group 'Rome – the world's most beautiful city'. Lots of tips, details of events, news and much more about Rome. The content of this group is open to everyone.

▶ www.gusto.com When you enter ‹Rome› in the search function, you'll be asked if you mean Rome/Italy or the Rome in Ohio or upstate New York. If you know the right answer to that, you'll find a good summary of attractions, restaurants and hotels.

▶ www.tripsay.com Questions and comments from others who have been there, and a good interactive hotel map that shows you the price.

TRAVEL TIPS

ARRIVAL

Rome has two airports. Scheduled flights, e.g. Alitalia from London and New York, British Airways from London, go to *Leonardo da Vinci* airport in *Fiumicino*, which lies 20 miles outside Rome. Charter and budget airlines such as Ryanair and Easyjet land at *Ciampino*, about 11 miles south-east of Rome.

Leonardo da Vinci: a taxi to the city centre costs approx. 50 euros. It's faster and cheaper to take a train: the *Leonardo Express* runs non-stop to Stazione Termini *(14 euros, tickets from the machines close to the platform | return from Termini to Fiumicino from platform 25 (beyond platform 24) | 5.52am–23.52pm every 30 min).*

Ciampino: a taxi to the city centre costs approx. 35 euros. Some airlines provide a bus service to Stazione Termini for 8 euros. The city buses will even take you there for 4 euros every 20 minutes.

Private airport shuttles are not always punctual and can be more expensive than taxis. Note: when you fly home, get to the airport at least two hours in advance to leave time for the security checks!

The *Autostrada del Sole* from Florence leads to the *Grande Raccordo Anulare (G.R.A.),* Rome's orbital motorway. Always follow the signs for *Roma centro*; otherwise you end up in the suburbs!

Most trains arrive at *Stazione Termini.* The trains that carry holidaymakers' cars stop at *Stazione Tiburtina.*

BANKS

All banks *(banca)* and savings banks *(cassa di risparmio)* have cashpoints (ATMs) and usually open *Mon–Fri 8.30am–1.30pm and 3–4pm.*

RESPONSIBLE TRAVEL

It doesn't take a lot to be environmentally friendly whilst travelling. Don't just think about your carbon footprint whilst flying to and from your holiday destination but also about how you can protect nature and culture abroad. As a tourist it is especially important to respect nature, look out for local products, cycle instead of driving, save water and much more. If you would like to find out more about eco-tourism please visit: *www.ecotourism.org*

BIKES & MOPEDS

Addresses for cycle hire: *Piazza di Spagna* (137 E1) (*ഥ E–F7*) or *Via del Pellegrino 82* (136 B4) (*ഥ D8*) and *Bici e baci* (140 C5) (*ഥ H7*) *(Via del Viminale 5 | www.bicibaci.com).* If you want to plunge into the Roman traffic on a moped, you can rent one from *Spagna Rent (Vicolo del Bottino 8 | exit Metro A: Spagna* (137 E1) (*ഥ E–F 6–7*) *| tel. 06 63 22 52 40 |)* or *Romarent (Vicolo dei Bovari 7a* (136 C5) (*ഥ D9*), *near Campo de' Fiori | tel. 06 68 95 55).*

From arrival to weather

Holiday from start to finish: the most important addresses and information for your trip to Rome

BUS, TRAM & METRO

A *BIT* ticket for bus or Metro costs 1 euro *(single trip, valid for 75 min)*, a day ticket 4 euros (3 days 11 euros, 7 days 16 euros). Buy them from an office of *ATAC* (the transport authority), e.g. in front of Stazione Termini (140 C5) (*ψ H8*), Piazza S. Silvestro (137 E2) (*ψ E7*) or at one of the many tobacconists and kiosks with the black, red and yellow *ATAC* sign. The tickets have to be stamped in the bus, Metro or tram!

Rome has only two Metro lines. *Linea A:* Battistini to Anagnina (south-eastern suburb, towards Castelli Romani) and *Linea B:* Rebibbia to EUR-Laurentina. Both run *Sun–Fri 5.30am–11.30pm, Sat 5.30–0.30am (Linea A at present only 5.30am–9pm due to construction work).* There are ticket machines at station entrances. You can buy the *Roma Metro-Bus* timetable for 6 euros in *ATAC* kiosks or at *www.atac.roma.it.* Details of individual routes at *http://infopoint.atac.roma.it.*

CAR HIRE

All the major car hire firms *(autonoleggio)* have branches at the two airports and in the city centre, e.g. *Hertz (tel. 199 11 22 11 in Italy | www.hertz.it), Avis (tel. 06 452 10 83 91 | www.avisauto noleggio.it), Europcar (tel. 199 30 70 30 | www.europcar.it | www.cheap-car-rental-reservations.net).*

CONSULATES & EMBASSIES

UK EMBASSY
British Embassy / Via XX Settembre 80a / 00187 Roma RM / tel. 06-4220 0001 / http://ukinitaly.fco.gov.uk/en/

US EMBASSY
Via Vittorio Veneto 121 / 00187 Rome, Italy / tel. 06-46741 / www.usembassy.it

CUSTOMS

Unlimited goods for personal use can be imported and exported without paying duties within states of the European Union. If you come from outside the EU, the

CURRENCY CONVERTER

£	€	€	£
1	1.10	1	0.90
3	3.30	3	2.70
5	5.50	5	4.50
13	14.30	13	11.70
40	44	40	36
75	82.50	75	67.50
120	132	120	108
250	275	250	225
500	550	500	450

$	€	€	$
1	0.70	1	1.40
3	2.10	3	4.20
5	3.50	5	7
13	9.10	13	18.20
40	28	40	56
75	52.50	75	105
120	84	120	168
250	175	250	350
500	350	500	700

For current exchange rates see www.xe.com

BUDGETING

Coffee	0.90 euros
	a cup of espresso standing at the counter
Ice cream	3 euros
	for a large portion
Water	1.50 euros
	for mineral water/cola
Stamp	65/85 cents
	for a letter sent within the EU/to North America
T-shirt	10 euros
	for a Rome t-shirt
Bus	1 euro
	for a single journey

duty-free allowances are: 1 litre of spirits or 2 litres of sparkling wine or 2 litres of fortified wine, and 4 litres of non-sparkling wine; 200 cigarettes or 250 grams of smoking tobacco or 100 cigarillos or 50 cigars, plus other goods with a maximum total value of 430 euros.

DRIVING

Italy's traffic regulations have become stricter, and fines are steep. The maximum blood alcohol level is 0.05%. Seat belts must be worn, and moped riders must have a helmet. The speed limit on three-lane motorways is 130 km/h (110 if it rains). Outside built-up areas cars must drive with their lights on. Remember to have a fluorescent jacket, which you need in case of breakdown when leaving the car outside built-up areas – the fine for not having one is 137 euros.

EMERGENCY

Police (Carabinieri): *tel. 112, 113*
Fire brigade: *tel. 115*

ACI breakdown service: *tel. 116*
Stolen cars: *Questura (Via Genova 2* (140 B6) *(🕮 G8)* | *tel. 0 64 68 61)*, where interpreters are available, or the nearest police or Carabinieri station.

GUIDED TOURS

How to see the sights of Rome:

ARCHEOBUS TO VIA APPIA
Daily departures 8.30, 9, 9.30, 10am and 3, 3.30, 4, 4.30pm | Piazza Cinquecento (Stazione Termini) (140 C5) *(🕮 H8)* | *day ticket to hop on and off as you please 10 euros, combined ticket Archeobus/Linea 110, valid for two days, 20 euros*
A cheap alternative (1 euro) to the Catacombs of Sebastian is the public bus no. 218 *(from S. Giovanni in Laterano)* (144 C3) *(🕮 J10)* or bus 118 *(from Piazzale Ostiense)* (143 E–F5) *(🕮 F13)*.

LINEA 110 – RED DOUBLE-DECKER
Daily departures 8.40am–7.40pm every 20 min | Piazza Cinquecento (Stazione Termini) (140 C5) *(🕮 H8)* | *day ticket to hop on and off as you please 10 euros, combined ticket Archeobus/Linea 110, for two days 20 euros*

ROME OPEN TOUR – GREEN DOUBLE-DECKER
Daily departures 9am–6.45pm every 25 min | Piazza Cinquecento (Stazione Termini) (140 C5) *(🕮 H8)* | *day ticket to hop on and off as you please 20 euros, for two days 25 euros | www.romeopentour.com*

ROMA CRISTIANA – PILGRIM LINE
The double-decker bus run by the Roman pilgrim organisation takes you to the seven pilgrimage churches and other Roman Catholic sights. *Daily departures 8.30am–7.30pm | Via della Conciliazione (St Peter's Square)* (138 B5) *(🕮 B7)* | *day*

ticket to hop on and off 17 euros, incl. public transport 19 euros, 3-day ticket 25 euros

LINES 116, 117, 118, 119

The INSIDER TIP best routes in Rome: *bus 116* takes you from Villa Borghese (Porta Pinciana) (140 A3–4) (*M F6*) to Via Veneto, Piazza del Parlamento, Corso Rinascimento, Corso Vittorio Emanuele, Campo de' Fiori and Gianicolo; *bus 117* links Piazza del Popolo (139 E3) (*M E6*), Piazza Venezia, Via dei Fori Imperiali, Colosseo and the Lateran basilica. *Bus 118* runs between Piazzale Ostiense (143 E–F5) (*M F13*), Aventino, Terme di Caracalla, Porta Sebastiano, Via Appia Antica and Via Appia Pignatelli. *Bus 119:* Piazza del Popolo (139 E3) (*M E6*) to Via Veneto. *Mon–Fri 8am–9pm, Sat 8am– midnight*

ROMACULTA

Art historians and archaeologists show you the city on wonderful individual guided walks, e. g. Roman Landmarks, Baroque Walks and Art in the Vatican. *Tel. 33 87 60 74 70 | www.romaculta.it*

ROMAMIRABILIA

Guided tours with an art historian, as well as gourmet and shopping tours. *Tel. 0 63 38 40 12 | www.romamirabilia.com*

HEALTH

Emergencies and ambulance: *tel. 118*
24-hour pharmacy:
Farmacia Internazionale: *Piazza dei Cinquecento (Stazione Termini) 51* (140 C5) (*M H8*) *and Via Cola di Rienzo 213* (138 B4) (*M C6*)
First aid *(pronto soccorso)* is free of charge in all hospitals. For citizens of the EU, the European insurance card EHIC entitles you to treatment (sometimes with additional fees). Visitors from North Ame-

rica and other non-EU countries should take out private insurance. Children's hospital *(Ospedale dei Bambini)*: *Piazza S. Onofrio* (142 B1) (*M B8*) *| tel. 0 66 85 91*

HOLIDAY TIMES

Many hotels, restaurants and shops are closed in early January and in the Italian holiday season, i.e. in the weeks around 15 August *(Ferragosto)*.

INFORMATION BEFORE YOU GO

ITALIAN STATE TOURIST BOARD

– 1, Princes Street | London W1B 2AY | tel. 020 74 08 12 54 | www.enit.it
– 630 Fifth Avenue · Suite 1565 / New York, New York 10111 / tel. 212 245-5618 / www.enit.it
– PO Box Q802 · QVB NSW 1230 / Level 4, 46 Market Street / Sydney NSW 2000 / Australia / tel. 02 9262 1666 / www.enit.it

INFORMATION IN ROME

INFO LINE & INFO PAVILIONS

INSIDER TIP The tourist authorities run an information service: *tel. 06 06 08, Mon–Sat 4–7pm,* for information in English about public transport, events and opening hours (see also *www.rome.info*). There are also tourist information pavilions: Castel Sant'Angelo *(Piazza Pia)* (138 C5) (*M C7*); Corso *(Via Minghetti)* (137 E3) (*M E8*); Via dei Fori Imperiali *opposite Forum Romanum)* (144 A2) (*M F9*); Stazione Termini *(by platform 24, entrance also from Via Giolitti 34)* (140 C6) (*M J8*); Piazza Sonnino *(Trastevere)* (143 D2) (*M D10*); Santa Maria Maggiore (140 C6) (*M H8*); Piazza Cinque Lune *(near Piazza Navona)* (136 C3) (*M D8*); Via Nazionale (Palazzo Esposizioni) (140 B6) (*M G8*)

TOURING CLUB ITALIANO

(139 E4) (*□ C6*) Advice for drivers, including traffic updates. *Via Giulio Cesare 98 | tel. 06 36 00 52 81 | www.touringclub. it | bus 280*

RAILWAYS (FS)

(140 C5) (*□ H8*) Timetable information *tel. 89 20 21 | www.ferroviedellostato. it,* reservations via travel agents in Rome and in Stazione Termini.

INTERNET & WIFI

Most large hotels have WiFi – *rete senza fili* in Italian – but charge for it. Thanks to *www.romawireless.com* you can

INSIDER TIP surf free of charge for an hour a day at about 20 of the nicest city squares, e.g. Campo de' Fiori, Piazza di Spagna, Fontana di Trevi, Campidoglio, Piazza Farnese, Circo Massimo and in parks such as Villa Borghese, Villa Ada, Villa Paganini and Villa Torlonia. Cafés with a WiFi service: *The Library (Vicolo della Cancelleria 7 | www.thelibrary.it)*, *Café Friends (Piazza Trilussa 34)* or *Good Bar (Via di San Dorotea 8–9)*. There are plenty of internet cafés in Rome, e.g. *Sistina Internet Point* (137 F2) (*□ F7*), which has about 15 terminals *(only 2.50 euros/hr)*, where you may also phone using Skype *(Via Zucchelli 1d/Via del Tritone)*, or *Globalservice* (143 D2) (*□ D10*),

WEATHER IN ROME

	Jan	Feb	March	April	May	June	July	Aug	Sept	Oct	Nov	Dec
Daytime temperatures in °C/°F												
	11/52	13/55	16/61	19/66	23/73	28/82	31/88	31/88	27/81	21/70	16/61	12/54
Nighttime temperatures in °C/°F												
	4/40	5/41	7/45	10/50	13/55	17/63	20/68	20/68	17/63	13/55	9/48	5/41
Sunshine hours/day												
	4	4	5	7	8	10	11	10	7	6	5	4
Precipitation days/month												
	8	9	8	8	7	4	2	2	5	8	10	10
Water temperature in °C/°F												
	14/57	13/55	13/55	14/57	17/63	21/70	23/73	24/75	23/73	20/68	18/64	15/59

a travel agency and internet café in Trastevere *(Piazza Sonnino 27)*.

LOST & FOUND

The city's lost property office *(Ufficio degli Oggetti Rinvenuti)* is in the Garbatella quarter in the *Circonvallazione Ostiense 191 (0)* *(₪ F14)* *(Mon–Fri 8.30am–1pm. Tue, Thu 3–5pm | tel. 06 67 69 32 14 | www.oggettismarriti@commune.roma. it | Metro B: Garbatella)*.

PHONE & MOBILE PHONE

To phone home, the code is *0044* for UK, *00353* for Ireland, then the local code without the first *0*. The country code for the USA and Canada is *001*. When phoning Italy from abroad, the code is *0039* – followed by the local code including the *0*. The Italian word for mobile phone is *cellulare* or *telefonino*. You'll get a signal everywhere in Rome, usually from the *TIM (Telecom Italiana Mobile)* network. Costs per minute within Italy are approx. 25 cents. If you want to use a landline, it's best to buy a phone card *(carta telecom no distance)* for 5, 10 or 20 euros at a tobacconist's and make the call from a public phone.
All phone numbers in Rome start with 06 – whether you make a call from within the city, from somewhere else in Italy or from abroad.

ROMA PASS

For 25 euros the *Roma Pass* gives you use of the Metro lines and all buses, free admission to two museums of your choice without queuing (not valid for the Vatican Museums) and discounts for other museums and exhibitions. The pass is on sale at all tourist information kiosks, ATAC offices, in Stazione

Termini and at Fiumicino airport. *www. romapass.it*.

TABACCHI

Bus tickets, salt and postage stamps? All of that and more is sold in tabacchi, which stock much more than tobacco, and could be regarded as Rome's most important shops. Look out for the black sign, usually on the wall of a house, with a white T.

TAXI

Taxi trips are not cheap, but the taximeters are calibrated properly and checked. The basic price is 3 euros. Supplements: night rate from 10pm 6 euros, Sundays and holidays 4.20 euros, 1 euro per piece of luggage. Tariff 1, inside the orbital motorway: 1.42 euros/km, tariff 2: 1.80 euros/km. From Fiumicino Airport expect to pay approx. 50 euros to the city centre, from Ciampino 35 euros. *Tel. 06 49 94, 06 66 45, 06 35 70 and 06 88 22*

THEFT

If you are a victim of theft, notify the nearest police or Carabinieri station or the *Questura* (police administration). Interpreters are available to record the details. *Via Genova 2 (140 B6)* *(₪ G8)* | *tel. 06 46 86 61 | Metro A: Repubblica, bus 60, 64, 70, 71*

TIPPING

Here are some suggestions for the right amount: porters get 1 euro per bag, chambermaids 1 euro per night or 3 euros per week, a hotel porter 1 euro. Give waiters 5–10 per cent depending on how satisfied you were. Taxi drivers expect nothing, but you can round up the amount if happy with the service.

USEFUL PHRASES ITALIAN

PRONUNCIATION

c, cc	before e or i like ch in "church", e.g. ciabatta, otherwise like k
ch, cch	like k, e.g. pacchi, che
g, gg	before e or i like j in "just", e.g. gente, otherwise like g in "get"
gl	like "lli" in "million", e.g. figlio
gn	as in "cognac", e.g. bagno
sc	before e or i like sh, e.g. uscita
sch	like sk in "skill", e.g. Ischia
z	at the beginning of a word like dz in "adze", otherwise like ts

An accent on an Italian word shows that the stress is on the last syllable.
In other cases we have shown which syllable is stressed by placing a dot below
the relevant vowel.

IN BRIEF

Yes/No/Maybe	Sì/No/Forse
Please/Thank you	Per favore/Grazie
Excuse me, please!	Scusa!/Mi scusi
May I ...?/Pardon?	Posso ...? / Come dice?/Prego?
I would like to .../Have you got ...?	Vorrei .../Avete ...?
How much is ...?	Quanto costa ...?
I (don't) like that	(Non) mi piace
good/bad	buono/cattivo/bene/male
broken/doesn't work	guasto/non funziona
too much/much/little/all/nothing	troppo/molto/poco/ tutto/niente
Help!/Attention!/Caution!	aiuto!/attenzione!/prudenza!
ambulance/police/fire brigade	ambulanza/polizia/vigili del fuoco
Prohibition/forbidden/danger/dangerous	divieto/vietato/pericolo/pericoloso
May I take a photo here/of you?	Posso fotografar La?

GREETINGS, FAREWELL

Good morning!/afternoon!/ evening!/night!	Buon giorno!/Buon giorno!/ Buona sera!/Buona notte!
Hello! / Goodbye!/See you	Ciao!/Salve! / Arrivederci!/Ciao!
My name is ...	Mi chiamo ...
What's your name?	Come si chiama?/Come ti chiami
I'm from ...	Vengo da ...

Parli italiano?

"Do you speak Italian?" This guide will help you to say the basic words and phrases in Italian.

DATE & TIME

Monday/Tuesday/Wednesday	lunedì/martedì/mercoledì
Thursday/Friday/Saturday	giovedì/venerdì/sabato
Sunday/holiday/ working day	domenica/(giorno) festivo/ (giorno) feriale
today/tomorrow/yesterday	oggi/domani/ieri
hour/minute	ora/minuto
day/night/week/month/year	giorno/notte/settimana/mese/anno
What time is it?	Che ora è? Che ore sono?
It's three o'clock/It's half past three	Sono le tre/Sono le tre e mezza
a quarter to four	le quattro meno un quarto/ un quarto alle quattro

TRAVEL

open/closed	aperto/chiuso
entrance/exit	entrata/uscita
departure/arrival	partenza/arrivo
toilets/ladies/gentlemen	bagno/toilette/signore/signori
(no) drinking water	acqua (non) potabile
Where is ...?/Where are ...?	Dov'è ...?/Dove sono ...?
left/right/straight ahead/back	sinistra/destra/dritto/indietro
close/far	vicino/lontano
bus/tram	bus/tram
taxi/cab	taxi/tassì
bus stop/cab stand	fermata/posteggio taxi
parking lot/parking garage	parcheggio/parcheggio coperto
street map/map	pianta/mappa
train station/harbour	stazione/porto
airport	aeroporto
schedule/ticket	orario/biglietto
supplement	supplemento
single/return	solo andata/andata e ritorno
train/track	treno/binario
platform	banchina/binario
I would like to rent ...	Vorrei noleggiare ...
a car/a bicycle	una macchina/una bicicletta
a boat	una barca
petrol/gas station	distributore/stazione di servizio
petrol/gas / diesel	benzina/diesel/gasolio
breakdown/repair shop	guasto/officina

FOOD & DRINK

Could you please book a table for tonight for four?	Vorrei prenotare per stasera un tavolo per quattro?
on the terrace/by the window	sulla terrazza/ vicino alla finestra
The menu, please/	La carta/il menù, per favore
Could I please have ...?	Potrei avere ...?
bottle/carafe/glass	bottiglia/caraffa/bicchiere
knife/fork/spoon/salt/pepper	coltello/forchetta/cucchiaio/sale/pepe
sugar/vinegar/oil/milk/cream/lemon	zucchero/aceto/olio/latte/panna/limone
cold/too salty/not cooked	freddo/troppo salato/non cotto
with/without ice/sparkling	con/senza ghiaccio/gas
vegetarian/allergy	vegetariano/vegetariana/allergia
May I have the bill, please?	Vorrei pagare/Il conto, per favore
bill/tip	conto/mancia

SHOPPING

Where can I find...?	Dove posso trovare ...?
I'd like .../I'm looking for ...	Vorrei .../Cerco ...
Do you put photos onto CD?	Vorrei masterizzare delle foto su CD?
pharmacy/shopping centre/kiosk	farmacia/centro commerciale/edicola
department store/supermarket	grandemagazzino/supermercato
baker/market/grocery	forno/ mercato/negozio alimentare
photographic items/newspaper shop/	articoli per foto/giornalaio
100 grammes/1 kilo	un etto/un chilo
expensive/cheap/price/more/less	caro/economico/prezzo/di più/di meno
organically grown	di agricoltura biologica

ACCOMMODATION

I have booked a room	Ho prenotato una camera
Do you have any ... left?	Avete ancora ...
single room/double room	una (camera) singola/doppia
breakfast/half board/	prima colazione/mezza pensione/
full board (American plan)	pensione completa
at the front/seafront/lakefront	con vista/con vista sul mare/lago
shower/sit-down bath/balcony/terrace	doccia/bagno/balcone/terrazza
key/room card	chiave/scheda magnetica
luggage/suitcase/bag	bagaglio/valigia/borsa

BANKS, MONEY & CREDIT CARDS

bank/ATM/pin code	banca/bancomat/ codice segreto
cash/credit card	in contanti/carta di credito
bill/coin/change	banconota/moneta/il resto

HEALTH

doctor/dentist/paediatrician	medico/dentista/pediatra
hospital/emergency clinic	ospedale/pronto soccorso/guardia medica
fever/pain/inflamed/injured	febbre/dolori/infiammato/ferito
diarrhoea/nausea/sunburn	diarrea/nausea/scottatura solare
plaster/bandage/ointment/cream	cerotto/fasciatura/pomata/crema
pain reliever/tablet/suppository	antidolorifico/compressa/supposta

POST, TELECOMMUNICATIONS & MEDIA

stamp/letter/postcard	francobollo/lettera/cartolina
I need a landline phone card/	Mi serve una scheda telefonica per la
I'm looking for a prepaid card for my	rete fissa/Cerco una scheda prepagata
mobile	per il mio cellulare
Where can I find internet access?	Dove trovo un accesso internet?
dial/connection/engaged	comporre/linea/occupato
socket/adapter/charger	presa/riduttore/caricabatterie
computer/battery/rechargeable battery	computer/batteria/accumulatore
internet address (URL)/e-mail address	indirizzo internet/indirizzo email
internet connection/wifi	collegamento internet/wi-fi
e-mail/file/print	email/file/stampare

LEISURE, SPORTS & BEACH

beach/bathing beach	spiaggia/bagno/stabilimento balneare
sunshade/lounger/cable car/chair lift	ombrellone/sdraio/funivia/seggiovia
(rescue) hut/avalanche	rifugio/valanga

NUMBERS

0	zero	15	quindici
1	uno	16	sedici
2	due	17	diciassette
3	tre	18	diciotto
4	quattro	19	diciannove
5	cinque	20	venti
6	sei	21	ventuno
7	sette	50	cinquanta
8	otto	100	cento
9	nove	200	duecento
10	dieci	1000	mille
11	undici	2000	duemila
12	dodici	10000	diecimila
13	tredici	½	un mezzo
14	quattordici	¼	un quarto

NOTES

FOR YOUR NEXT HOLIDAY ...

MARCO POLO TRAVEL GUIDES

MARCO POLO
With ROAD ATLAS & PULL-OUT MAP
LAKE GARDA
E BALDO WITH MOUNTAIN BIKE
n Malcesine takes bikes too
SSES" IN SALÒ
colate "bacero"
Travel with Insider Tips

MARCO POLO
With STREET ATLAS & PULL-OUT MAP
NEW YORK
OWS, WILD FLOWERS AND SKYSCRAPERS
c: the High Line in Chelsea
AIL UN CLOUD NINE
op bar at 230 Fifth Street
Travel with Insider Tips

MARCO POLO
With ROAD ATLAS & PULL-OUT MAP
FRENCH RIVIERA
NICE, CANNES & MONACO
SPECTACULAR GRAND CANYON DU VERDON
Breath-taking scenery that takes some beating
SNIFFING THE AIR
The perfume manufacturers of Grasse
Travel with Insider Tips
www.marcooolouk.com

MARCO POLO
With ROAD ATLAS & PULL-OUT MAP
ALLORCA
AN FLAIR IN THE MEDITERRANEAN
allorca's most beautiful beach
E ...IN" CROWD MEET
fonda in Deià
Travel with Insider Tips

MARCO POLO
With STREET ATLAS & PULL-OUT MAP
BERLIN
A STUNNING ISLAND JUST FOR ART
Showcasing treasures from around the world
STAY COOL AT NIGHT
scene sets the trend
Travel with Insider Tips
www.marcopolouk.com

- PACKED WITH INSIDER TIPS
- BEST WALKS AND TOURS
- FULL-COLOUR PULL-OUT MAP
  AND STREET ATLAS

STREET ATLAS

The green line ▬▬▬ indicates the Walking tours (p. 110–115)

All tours are also marked on the pull-out map

Photo: View from the Aventine hill

Exploring Rome

The map on the back cover shows how the area has been sub-divided

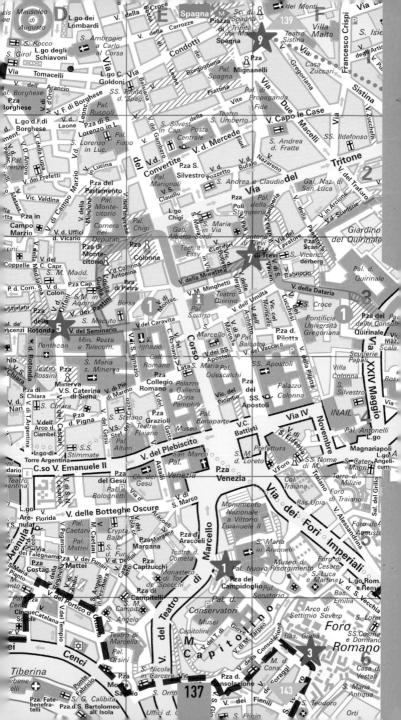

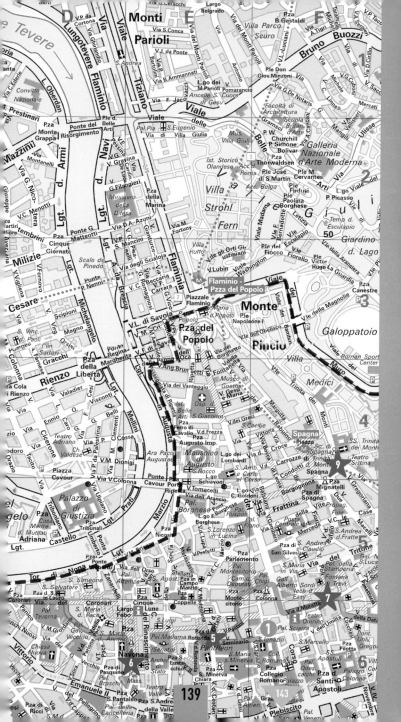

141

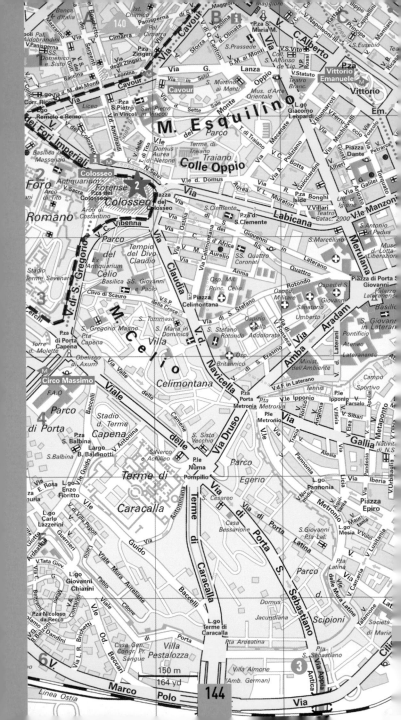

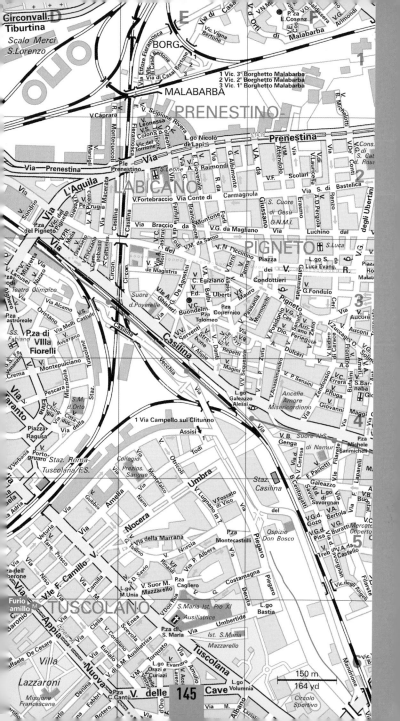

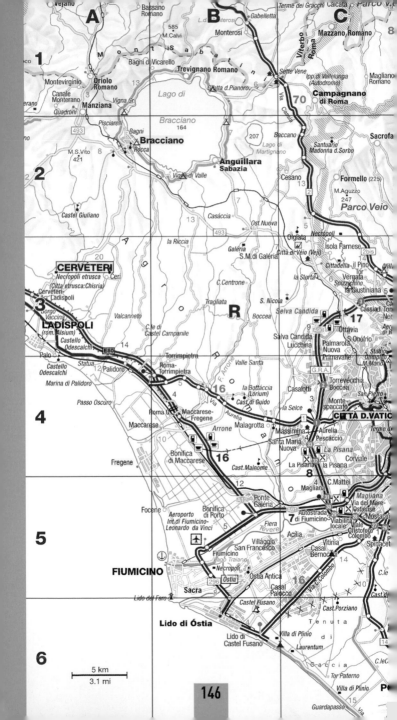

The index includes a selection of the streets and squares shown in the street atlas

KEY TO STREET ATLAS

German		English		French / Italian
Autobahn / Motorway (Freeway)				Autoroute / Autostrada
Vierspurige Straße / Road with four lanes				Route à quatre voies / Strada a quattro corsie
Bundes-/Fernstraße / Federal / trunk road				Route fédérale / nationale / Strada statale /di grande comunicazione
Hauptstraße / Main road				Route principale / Strada principale
Fußgängerzone - Einbahnstraße / Pedestrian zone - One way road				Zone piétonne - Rue à sens unique / Zona pedonale - Via a senso unico
Eisenbahn mit Bahnhof / Railway with station				Chemin de fer avec gare / Ferrovia con stazione
U-Bahn / Underground (railway)				Métro / Metropolitana
Buslinie - Straßenbahn / Bus-route - Tramway				Ligne d'autocar - Tram / Linea d'autobus - Tram
Information - Jugendherberge / Information - Youth hostel				Information - Auberge de jeunesse / Informazioni - Ostello della gioventù
Kirche - Sehenswerte Kirche / Church - Church of interest				Église - Église remarquable / Chiesa - Chiesa di notevole interesse
Synagoge - Moschee / Synagogue - Mosque				Synagogue - Mosquée / Sinagoga - Moschea
Polizeistation - Postamt / Police station - Post office				Poste de police - Bureau de poste / Posto di polizia - Ufficio postale
Krankenhaus / Hospital				Hôpital / Ospedale
Denkmal - Funk- oder Fernsehturm / Monument - Radio or TV tower				Monument - Tour d'antennes / Monumento - Pilone radio o TV
Theater - Taxistand / Theatre - Taxi rank				Théâtre - Station taxi / Teatro - Posteggio di tassi
Feuerwache - Schule / Fire station - School				Puste de pompiers - École / Guardia del fuoco - Scuola
Freibad - Hallenbad / Open air - / Indoor swimming pool				Piscine en plein air - Piscine couverte / Piscina all'aperto - Piscina coperta
Öffentliche Toilette - Ausflugslokal / Public toilet - Restaurant				Toilette publique - Restaurant / Gabinetto pubblico - Ristorante
Parkhaus - Parkplatz / Indoor car park - Car park				Parking couvert - Parking / Autosilo - Area di parcheggio
Stadtspaziergänge / Walking tours				Promenades en ville / Passeggiate urbane
MARCO POLO Highlight				MARCU POLO Highlight

INDEX

All sights and destinations mentioned in this guide as well as some important streets and squares are listed in this index. Page numbers in bold refer to the main entry.